Great Salespeople Never Die

Never Die

They Just Go Out of Commission

Jerry "Mr. Cutco" Otteson

Printed in the U.S.A.

"The Happy Norwegian" Publications

Great Salespeople Never Die

They Just Go Out of Commission

Second Edition

GREAT SALESPEOPLE NEVER DIE - SECOND EDITION.
Copyright© July 2012.

Published by
"The Happy Norwegian" Publications
The Heritage
2600 S. Heritage Woods Drive, Apt. C304
Appleton, WI 54915
For quantity discounts, contact the publisher

Printed by
PrintSource Plus, Inc.
1314 W. College Avenue
Appleton, WI 54914

Printed in the United States of America

ISBN: 978-1-4675-3975-3

Library of Congress Catalog Number: 2012944107

First Printing: July 2012

08 07 06 05 04 6 5 4 3 2 1

Acknowledgements

I want to thank Kathy Dreyer, who edited and typed this book for me. SHE IS THE BEST and I could not have done it without her. Kathy is the assistant to our Downtown Appleton Rotary Club and she does an outstanding job!

Steve Steinbach and his printing company, PrintSource Plus, printed my book. Steve did a wonderful job and I am proud of him - A+!

Thanks to Nifty Nick of PrintSource for the layout of the book. He did an excellent job with the layout.

Nancy Miller for proofreading my book, she is great.

And all of my friends that encouraged me to write this book. I have an "Attitude of Gratitude" to all of you!

Dedication

I dedicate this book to my beautiful, great, feisty wife Donna Jean Otteson. My Donna was a wonderful wife for 42 years. At least 70% of my success as a CUTCO Cutlery division manager was because of Donna. She was a perfect role model to all of our young managers and their wives or husbands. Her judgment was better than mine. <u>I not only loved Donna, but I also liked her.</u> Donna was much smarter than me.

Jerry and Donna's Wedding Photo – April 3, 1965

Donna and Jerry on their honeymoon
in Acapulco, Mexico

My Donna was a classy lady. A friend of ours asked Donna what she thought of this lady that we all knew. Donna answered, <u>"She's not my favorite."</u> That is a lot classier and better than saying that she did not like her. <u>Your life is much richer if you knew Donna.</u>

<u>At her funeral, someone asked me which were my stepdaughters. I told them that we did not have stepdaughters — we have daughters.</u> No one could have done as good a job as Donna in raising our seven daughters. We are very proud of our family. <u>Our seven daughters are the precious jewels of my life.</u>

Donna played in the Grandmother Tournament in 1980 at Riverview County Club, she won. Donna did not golf until we got married – she was 37. Donna was a very good golfer. <u>She was good at everything</u>. The best thing I ever did for my Donna that money would buy was to join Riverview Country Club.

Our daughters at home after Donna's funeral.
Top row: Lori, Becky, Heidi
Bottom row: Jerry, Patti, Stacy, Debby and Toni

Bernice saved me in Cutco many, many times. I married Bernice Myhra at First Lutheran Church in Fargo, North Dakota on August 26, 1950. Bernice was a pure Norwegian. Bernice was a perfect Cutco wife. She played the piano and organ very, very well, I loved Bernice.

SAINT JEROME OF CUTCO
1926 ~ 2026

Jerry is looking in the window at desserts in Turkey. His willpower is sensational. According to this, he's been eating all the wrong foods for 85 years. He had a chance to be thin, but he turned it down.

Two Wonderful Things

Two wonderful things will happen to you when you read this book:

1. You will learn a lot.
2. You will laugh many times.

If you are good now, you can be great by reading this book. If you are great now, you can be even greater after reading this book. You and I can't stay the same even if we try. So get better!

Some Like Me, Some Don't

Some people are going to like me and some are not, so I might as well be me. At least then, I will know that the people who like me, like me for who I am.

I Love Myself

I love myself, I think I am grand
I go to the show, And hold my hand
I put my arms around my waist
And when I get fresh I slap my face

Love

Love like you have never been hurt.

I love you. You love me. God loves us. We like that.

Love in Your Heart

When you have love in your heart, everyone around you will find joy in your presence.

Dance

Dance like nobody is watching.

Be Happy

The best time to be happy is now. Be happy.

Best

Be the best you can be.

Yesterday
If what you did yesterday still looks big to you, then you have not done much today.

A Friend
A friend is one who knows all about you and won't go away.

Do You Know?
Do you know my friend Ferris?
He is that big wheel at the fair.

Tough People
Tough times do not last. Tough people do.

Happiness
Happiness is not the belief that we do not need to change. It is the realization that we can.

Love Me
Love me when I least deserve it because that is when I really need it.

My Life
My life has been an incredible adventure. Life is good.

Courage
Courage does not always roar. Sometimes courage is the little voice at the end of the day that says, "I'll try again tomorrow."

Mind
A human mind, once opened to a new idea, never returns to its former dimensions

No Respect
We have a friend that gets no respect. His insurance company sent him half a calendar.

Show Me
Show me your friends and I'll show you your future.

Attitude
Attitude is the only thing we have complete control over.

You Can't
The only one who can tell you "you can't" is you. And you don't have to listen.

Betray
If someone betrays you once, it's his fault. If he betrays you twice, it's your fault.

Great Minds
Great minds discuss ideas. Average minds discuss events. Small minds discuss people.

Ends
You can't make both ends meet sitting on one.

USA Today
USA Today has come out with a new survey. Apparently, 3 out of 4 people make up 75% of the population.

The Four Stages of Life
You believe in Santa Claus.
You do not believe in Santa Claus.
You are Santa Claus.
You look like Santa Claus.

Nice Matters
There are not many things more important than nice.

Never Quit
When you are wrestling with a gorilla, do not quit when you get discouraged. Do not quit until the gorilla gets discouraged.

Old Friends
New friends I cherish and treasure their worth,
But old friends, to me, are the salt of the earth.
Friends are like garments that everyone wears
New ones are needed for dress-up affairs.

But when we're at leisure, we're more apt to choose
The clothes that we purchased with last season's shoes,
Things we grow used to are things we love best,
The ones we are certain have weathered the test.
And isn't it true (since we're talking of friends)
That new ones bring pleasure when everything blends.
Like when we want someone who thinks as we do,
And who fits, as I mentioned like last season's shoes
We turn to the friends who have stuck through the years
Who echo our laughter and dry all our tears.
They know every weakness and fault we possess
But somehow forget them in friendships caress.

Some Tips for Making Your Life a Little Better

Sit in silence for ten minutes each day and think good thoughts.
Live with energy, enthusiasm, and empathy.
Make time for meditation and prayer.
Spend time with people over 70 and under the age of 6.
Try to make someone else smile every day.
Clear clutter from your house, your car, and your desk.
Do not waste your precious energy on gossip and negative thoughts about things you can't control.
Realize that life is a school and you are here to learn.
Know that problems will appear and fade away.
Eat breakfast like a queen, lunch like a princess, and supper like a college kid with a maxed-out credit card.
Laugh every single chance you get.
Life is not fair . . . but it is still good.
Life is far too short to waste time hating someone.
Do not take yourself so seriously.
You do not have to win every argument.
Make peace with your past so it won't spoil the present.
Don't compare your life to anyone else's life.
Nobody is in charge of your happiness but you.
When a so-called disaster occurs, ask yourself if it will even matter in five years.
Forgive everyone for everything.
What other people think of you is nobody's business.
However good or bad a situation is . . . it will change.
Stay in touch with friends.

Get rid of anything that isn't useful, beautiful, or joyful.
Envy is a total waste of your time.
Always believe that the best is yet to come.
No matter how you feel, get up, dress up, and show up.
Always do the right thing no matter what.
Call your family often and tell them you love them.
Every single night tell God you are thankful for something.
Believe that you are too blessed to be stressed.
You have only one ride through life, so make the most of it.

Happy People Live Longer?
Could happiness be the key to a long, or at least longer, life?
Maybe, researchers say.

In a study from the UK, older people who said they were happy,
even for a little while, were less likely to die over a five-year peri-
od. And the happier they were, the longer they lived. Overall, the
results showed that older people who reported feeling happiest
had a 35% lower risk of dying during the study than those who
were least happy. The study followed more than 3,800 people
in the UK aged 52 to 79 for five years. It was done as part of the
longest-running British study on aging.

Earlier studies have looked at happiness and longevity by asking
people to recall their emotional state. This study asked people
to rate their feelings of happiness and anxiety at different points
throughout the day. Researchers found that people who reported feeling happiest had a 35% lower risk of dying during the
study than people who were least happy

The study researchers caution that the results do not show a
cause-and-effect relationship between happiness and longer life.
Instead, they say, momentary happiness may relate to biologi-
cal processes or other behavioral factors that could explain the
increased survival odds. They do say, however, that the findings
emphasize the importance of emotional well-being for older
people.

The results were reported in the *Proceedings of the National
Academy of Sciences.*

A Friend Does Most or All of These ...

(A)ccepts you as you are
(B)elieves in you
(C)alls you just to say "hi"
(D)oesn't give up on you
(E)nvisions the whole of you (even the unfinished parts)
(F)orgives your mistakes
(G)ives unconditionally
(H)elps you
(I)nvites you over
(J)ust "be" with you
(K)eeps you close at heart
(L)oves you for who you are
(M)akes a difference in your life
(N)ever judges
(O)ffers support
(P)icks you up
(Q)uiets your fears
(R)aises your spirits
(S)ays nice things about you
(T)ells you the truth when you need to hear it
(U)nderstands you
(V)alues you
(W)alks beside you
(X)-plans things you don't understand
(Y)ells when you don't listen
(Z)aps you back to reality

Rewards

If you plant goodness, you will reap friends.
If you plant humility, you will reap greatness.
If you plant perseverance, you will reap contentment.
If you plant consideration, you will reap perspective.
If you plant hard work, you will reap success.
If you plant forgiveness, you will reap reconciliation.
So, be careful what you plant now, it will determine what you will reap later.

It Couldn't Be Done

Somebody said that it couldn't be done. But he, with a chuckle, replied that maybe it couldn't, but he would be one who wouldn't say so "till he tried." So he buckled right in with the trace of a grin on his face. If he worried, he hid it. He started to sing as he tackled the thing that couldn't be done, and he did it.

Somebody scoffed: "Oh, you'll never do that; at least no one ever has done it." But he took off his coat and took off his hat, and the first thing he knew, he'd begun it. With the lift of his chin and a bit of a grin, without any doubting, he started to sing as he tackled the thing that couldn't be done, and he did it.

There are thousands to tell you it cannot be done, there are thousands to prophesy sure failure; there are thousands to point out to you, one by one, the dangers that wait to assail you. But just buckle right in with a bit of a grin, then take off your coat and go to it; just start in to sing as you tackle the thing that cannot be done, and you'll do it.

Deaf

People who may be deaf to your words are not going to be blind to your actions.

Intention

The smallest good is much better than the greatest intention.

It Is in You

To enjoy happiness, you must create it. Joy is not in things . . . it is in you!

10 Things to Remember

1. The value of time.
2. The success of perseverance.
3. The pleasure of working.
4. The dignity of simplicity.
5. The worth of character.
6. The power of kindness.
7. The obligation of duty.
8. The influence of example.

9. The wisdom of economy.
10. The virtue of patience.

Billy Graham
Hot heads and cold hearts never solve anything.

I Cried
I cried when I had no shoes until I saw a man that had no feet.

Surprises
I do like surprises. When I wake up, it is always a surprise.

Believe
Believe in people <u>before</u> they succeed. Help them win.

At the Top
There is always room at the top.

Appeasement
Winston Churchill said, "Appeasement is when you continue to feed the crocodiles and hope he eats you last!"

They Do Not Beat Anybody
This couple was getting a divorce and they had only one little boy, and the judge was trying to decide who the boy should live with. The judge said, "Do you want to live with your mother?" The boy said, "NO." The Judge asked him why not. The boy replied, "Because she beats me." The judge asked, "Do you want to live with your father?" The boy said, "NO." The judge then asked him why not. The boy replied, "He beats me too." The judge said to the little boy, "Who do you want to live with?' <u>The boy said, "I want to live with the Minnesota Vikings - - they don't beat anybody."</u>

I Have a New Rule
I only go to parties I am invited to, so I go to fewer parties then I did before.

Yesterday

Yesterday, I had 3 orders:
1. Get out!
2. Stay out!
3. And never come back.

Your Children

Your children will do what you do. They will not do what you say.

Live Below

Live below your means. Do not owe anyone.

Yesterday

Yesterday is a cancelled check.
Tomorrow is a promissory note.
Today is the only cash you have so spend it wisely

Be A

Be a dream releaser.

Be Better

Help someone else be better. Invest in people.

Satchel Paige

Satchel Page said, "How old would you be _if_ you did not know how old you was?"

How to Know You Are Growing Older

Everything hurts and what doesn't hurt doesn't work.
The gleam in your eye is from the sun hitting your bifocals.
You feel like the night before and you haven't been anywhere.
Your little black book contains only names ending in M.D.
You get winded playing cards.
You join a health club and don't go.
You know all the answers, but nobody asks you the questions.
You look forward to a dull evening.
You need glasses to find your glasses.
You turn out the lights for economic rather than
    romantic reasons.
You sit in a rocking chair and can't get it going.

Your knees buckle but your belt won't.
Your back goes out more than you do.
You have too much room in the house and not enough in the medicine chest.
You sink your teeth in a steak and they stay there.

Makes You Think

A young lady with a raised glass of water confidently walked around the room while leading and explaining stress management to an audience. Everyone knew she was going to ask the ultimate question, 'half empty or half full?'

She fooled them all . . . "How heavy is this glass of water?" she inquired with a smile.
Answers called out ranged from 8 oz. to 20 oz.

She replied, "The absolute weight doesn't matter. It depends on how long I hold it.
"If I hold it for a minute, that's not a problem.
"If I hold it for an hour, I'll have an ache in my right arm.
"If I hold it for a day, you'll have to call an ambulance.
"In each case, it's the same weight, but the longer I hold it, the heavier it becomes." She continued, "and that's the way it is with stress. If we carry our burdens all the same, sooner or later, as the burden becomes increasingly heavy, we won't be able to carry on.
"As with the glass of water, you have to put it down for a while and rest before holding it again. When we're refreshed, we can carry on with the burden – holding stress longer and better each time practiced. So, as early in the evening as you can, put all your burdens down. Don't carry them through the evening and into the night…. Pick them up tomorrow."

Had Trouble

Have you ever had trouble remembering names? I used to have trouble remembering names, but then I took this Sam Carnage course and have had no trouble ever since!

Starbuck, Minnesota

Two bits, four bits, six bits, a dollar.
Everyone from Starbuck stand up and holler!

You

You can do it!

Grow Up

You grow up the day you have your first real laugh at yourself.

Hold On

Hold on to your dreams.

Many People

Many people will walk in and out of your life but only true friends will leave footprints in your heart.

Moby Dick

I'm so optimistic I'd go after Moby Dick in a rowboat and take the tarter sauce with me.

Keep On

Keep on keeping on.

Everything

Everything is going to be all right.

Spend

Spend less than you make.

It Is Not

It is not how you have started in life that counts. It is how you finish.

Amazing

You are amazing – do not forget this. You have what it takes.

I Like Me

I like me. If you and I do not like ourselves, nobody else will like us.

Do Your Best
Do your best every day.

You Are in Front
If you get kicked in the rear, it means you are in front.

Never, Never
Never spend time with small-minded people.

Are You?
Are you part of the problem or part of the solution?

The Older I Get
The older I get the less judgmental I am.

The Eyes of Love
See people through the eyes of love.

Independently Wealthy
I used to be independently wealthy. <u>Now I am only independent</u>.

Only Place
The only place success comes before work is in the dictionary.

Great Marriage
If you have a great marriage, nothing else matters. I had two great marriages. They could not have been better. <u>I married up twice.</u>

Do Not
Do not fight battles that do <u>not</u> matter.

Make You Feel
No one can make you feel inferior without your permission.

Blue
Whenever I feel blue, I just start to breathe again.

Happiness
Happiness is a voyage, not a destination. There is no better time to be happy than now.

Norway – The Promised Land
I have been in Norway hundreds of times in my mind and four times in reality.

High Maintenance
My Donna often said that I was high maintenance, but that the fringe benefits were well worth it.

A Smile
A smile is the shortest distance between two people.

Enjoy Life
If we are ever to enjoy life, now is the time – not tomorrow or next year. Today should always be our most important day.

Most Important Day of the Year
May 17th is Norway's Constitution Day, National Day, or Syttende Mai. Please put your hand over your heart.

Admire
Among those whom I like or admire I can find no common denominator, <u>but among those who I love I can . . . they all make me laugh.</u>

It Was
It was so windy in Appleton the other day if I wasn't so fat I would have blown away.

Mark Twain
Humor is mankind's greatest blessing.

Boomerang
What do you call a boomerang that doesn't work? A stick.

Only Young Once
We are young only once and if we do it right, that is enough.

Within Us
What lies behind us and what lies before us are small matters compared to what lies within us.

You Will Never
Do not take life too seriously. You will never get out of it alive.

Of Course
Of course I do not look busy. I did it right the first time.

Eat Dessert First
Life is short. Eat your dessert first.

Wrinkles
Wrinkles should only indicate where smiles have been.

Integrity
With integrity, nothing else counts. Without integrity, nothing else counts.

Life
It is a funny thing about life; if you refuse to accept anything but the best, you very often get it.

You Might as Well
You might as well laugh at these jokes. They are not going to get any better.

No Mercy
When you are giving a talk and there is very little applause, say, "No mercy, applause please!"

Best Seat in the Room
Before you give a talk ask the people in the back of the room if they can hear you. If they can't, they have the best seat in the room.

Ignorance Versus Apathy
A college professor asked the following question on an exam, "What is the difference between ignorance and apathy?" He had

to give an A+ to Ole, his student, who answered, "I do not know and I do not care."

Judgment
Good judgment comes from experience and a lot of that comes from bad judgment.

Trouble
If you don't learn to laugh at trouble, you won't have anything to laugh at when you are old.

Grateful
I am very grateful every day.

Energy
Kids are like old people with energy.

Kids
I hear some Cutco managers call Cutco sales reps "kids." Kids are baby goats. Cutco sales reps are young Cutco champions.

Always
Always borrow money from a pessimist. They won't expect it back!

Bartender
A man walks into a bar and orders three doubles, then quickly downs one right after the other. As he starts the third, he orders three more. The bartender says, "You know, man, that's not good for you." "I know, particularly with what I have." "Why, what do you have?" "One dollar."

Not Sure
I used to be indecisive, now I'm not sure.

Slow Learners
Norwegians are slow learners. But we forget fast, once we learn.

College Reunion
I went to my college reunion and they had gotten so old they did not remember me.

Check Up
We all need a daily check up from the neck up to avoid stinkin' thinkin' which ultimately leads to hardening of the attitudes.

David and Goliath
They said to David, "Goliath is so big we can't beat him." David said, "He is so big, we can't miss him!"

Common Sense
Common sense and a sense of humor are the same thing moving at different speeds. A sense of humor is just common sense dancing.

Settle
If you settle for less than you deserve, you will get even less than you settled for.

Interrupt
If your work speaks for itself, do not interrupt.

Teenage Girl
A teenage girl ran to her father and said, "Daddy, Ronald wants me to marry him. Should I accept?" Her father peered over his newspaper and said, "Go ask your mother. She made a better decision than I did."

Workaholic
Why was the workaholic's national convention cancelled? They were all working.

Attitude
The most important word in the English language is - attitude.

Glass Overflowing
Some think a glass is half empty. Some think the glass is half full. I see the glass as overflowing.

Better

To feel better, you have to think better.
Whatever you do get better at it.

Behave

You behave yourself to success.

Count Your Blessings

Do the math. Count your blessings.

Grudge

A grudge is a heavy thing to carry.

A Bad Attitude

The biggest handicap in the world is a bad attitude.

$20.00 Fine

There will be a $20.00 fine for whining.

Stronger

What does not kill you will make you stronger.

Best Compliment

The best compliment you can give anyone – you are good
enough to be a Norwegian.

Norwegian Twice as Smart

Why is a Norwegian living in Appleton, Wisconsin twice as smart
as a Norwegian living in New York City? A Norwegian in Appleton knows the location of New York City. A Norwegian in New
York City does not know where Appleton, Wisconsin is.

Do Not

Do not give up on your dreams or your dreams will give up on
you.

How Many People

It's not how many mountains we climb that matters but rather
how many people we take along with us.

Love What You Do
Love what you do or do something else.

Never
I have never seen a monument erected to a pessimist.

How Do You Know That, Jerry?
Answer – I stay awake at the meetings.

My Father
My father did not tell me how to live. He lived and let me watch him do it.

My Life 1926-2026
I was born August 7, 1926 on a farm near Starbuck, Minnesota. I ran away a lot when I was 4, 5 and 6 years old. That is when I started my love of traveling.

7 Daughters
People ask me how old our daughters are. I reply, "It's hard to tell. It changes every day!"

Everything
Everything turns out for the best even when it does not seem so at the time.

I Was So Poor
I was so poor that my dad painted black x's on my feet and told me they were shoelaces.

Greatest Gift
My father gave me the greatest gift anyone could give another person. He believed in me.

If
If I had told my dad that I was quitting high school until I "find myself," he would have hit me on the head and said, "You are no longer lost."

Heart
I left my heart in Starbuck, Minnesota.

Roots and Wings
The two most important things parents can give their children
are "roots and wings."

Inconsistent
Man: You're inconsistent!" Wife: "Not all the time!"

Jail
Starbuck, Minnesota is so small, it does not even have a jail. If
someone commits a crime, he has to stand in the corner.

75 Years Ago
75 years ago from the issue of August 13, 1936 Starbuck, Minnesota newspaper, "Jerome Otteson, son of Mr. and Mrs. N. J.
Otteson, entertained a group of friends Friday afternoon on the
occasion of his 10th birthday."

Smart
I was so smart, my teacher was in my class for 5 years.

If
If you can't get along with yourself, you can't get along
with others.

My Father
My word is my bond. I learned this from my father.

Hugged
Have you hugged your Norwegian today?

Dependable
I am so dependable, it is scary!

Lost a Lot of Weight
I have lost so much weight that I am down to one scale.

I Went to the Doctor

I went to the doctor and he said, "Jerry, you have to lose weight." I went back to the doctor 60 days later and he said to me, "Jerry, you have to go off the diet. The only thing that is left is muscle."

30 Day Diet

I have been on this new 30-day diet but all I have lost so far is 30 days.

All Over the World

I have looked all over the world <u>to find just one dumb Norwegian</u>. I could not find even one dumb Norwegian. A friend of mine asked, "Have you looked in the mirror recently?"

Healthy

The people were so healthy in my hometown of Starbuck, Minnesota they had to shoot Ole to start a cemetery.

Norwegian Carpool

How do Norwegians carpool? They meet at work.

Greatest Sin

The greatest sin in the world is giving up.

My Favorite Song

My favorite song is *Don't Worry, Be Happy*.

Three Types of People

There are three types of people in the world:
Those that make things happen
Those who watch things happen
Those who have no idea what happened

Today

Today is the tomorrow you worried about yesterday.

Arguments
You can end any argument with just four little words – maybe you are right.

Eagles
You can't soar with the eagles if you cluck with the chickens.

Mistakes
You should learn from the mistakes of others. You can't live long enough to make them all yourself.

Tomorrow's Success
Today's success was yesterday's decision. Tomorrow's success is today's decision.

Success
If you are nice to people, you are already a success.

Lost
I get lost in a phone booth.

North Dakota
Stay in North Dakota. Custer was healthy when he left.

Rabbits
I used to be so fast, I ran down rabbits just for the exercise.

Doctor
Never go to a doctor whose office plants have died.

Roll Up
Roll up your pants legs. It is too late to save your shoes.

Nothing
Say nothing and stick to your story.

Encourage Someone
Encourage someone every day or better yet encourage 2, 3 or 4 people every day.

People

Make people feel good about themselves. Be free with compliments. One compliment can change a life. The power of an encouraging word is powerful.

Bumper Sticker

Donna gave me a bumper sticker that said, "Pray for me, I married a Norwegian."

10 Ways on "How to Be Great in Life" (by Dennis Episcopo)

1. Have faith
2. Marry right
3. Be likable
4. Have hope
5. Be positive automatically
6. Never give up
7. Do not get a big head
8. Love yourself
9. Bring something to the table
10. Learn how to love

Push-Ups

I am up to two consecutive push-ups. It is all up to you.

Special Diet

Of course, you heard about the guy who went on a special diet, nothing but powdered foods for two months. Then he got caught in a thundershower and gained 20 pounds in 5 minutes.

Casey Stengel

Casey Stengel said that 90% of our work is 50% mental.

Starbuck, Minnesota

Starbuck, Minnesota is where all the woman are beautiful, the men are strong and all the children are extra intelligent.

Alligator

Never insult an alligator until after you have crossed the river.

Gem of the Day
An ad in the local paper read, "For sale: complete set of Encyclopedia Britannica. Never used. My wife knows everything."

Exercise
I do not exercise anymore since I pulled a muscle while taking a nap.

Rainbows
Rainbows are my favorite color.

Laugh and Cry
If you want to be great in life you have to know how to laugh and how to cry.

Life
We believe that life is measured in memories not years.

Longest Journey
The longest journey you will ever take is the 18 inches from your head to your heart.

Conviction
What convinces us is conviction.

Bad Things
Bad things don't happen because you care, they happen when you don't care.

Look Out
If you don't look out for others, who will look out for you?

Realize
Realize how great you really are.

We Can't
We can't move ahead if we are trying to get even.

Too Busy Trying
If you are too busy to help those around you, you are too busy.

Human Being
Being a good human being is good business.

Dreams
Follow your dreams and enjoy the trip.

Life
Life is about turning the things you really want into the things you've done.

Courage
One person with courage makes a majority.

Depth
The only difference between a rut and a grave is the depth.

Loafing
I am not loafing; I work so fast I'm always done.

Crime
Crime would not pay if the government ran it.

Poor
I was so poor when my richest uncle died and when they read his will, I owed him $2,000.

Good, Better, Best
Good, better, best. Never, never rest till good is your better and your better is your best.

Neurotic
A neurotic is a person that is self-employed and can't get along with his boss.

Mark Twain
I am an old man and have a great many troubles but most of them never happened.

Farmers

If you complain about farmers, do not talk with your mouth full.

Die Young

I am too old to die young.

Amazing Grace

This letter was written to me by our granddaughter Grace from London, Canada. Her teacher asked her class to write an article on, "To learn from people around you."

"Every year a few times, I go visit my grandparents in Wisconsin. My grandpa is always telling me important facts. I have no clue how many valuable lessons I have learned from him. He told me to be nice to people and they will be nice back and to never give up. That got me someplace. He always makes me feel good when he tells me how special I am to him. So to people I love and care about, I do the same thing because I know how it makes me feel. I have learned many other things from him, but that would take forever so, this is who I learn the most from about valuable lessons in life."

We Were So Poor

We were so poor, my dad gave me a penny if I did not eat my dinner then he took it back because I did not clean my plate.

Look Back

Do not look back – it is a waste of time.

Sleep

Without enough sleep, we all become tall two-year-olds.

Do Not

Do not be around anyone that does not make you feel better.

Weight Watchers

I have been on the Weight Watchers diet for a month and have gained 12 pounds. I did not know that 5 fish and 2 pounds of beef was a week's supply.

Hub Caps
I used to live in such a tough neighborhood they used to steal hub caps, <u>from moving cars.</u>

On My Way
I do not know where I am going, but I am on my way.

Japanese Food
Japanese food is good if you like bait.

Donna and Bernice
<u>I made the living, and Donna and Bernice made the living worthwhile.</u>

Bumper Sticker
I have a bumper sticker on my car, "My favorite two football teams are the Green Bay Packers and whoever is playing the Bears."

Vince Lombardi
When you get into the end zone, act like you have been there before.

Broke
I have been broke but I have never been poor.

From What We
From what we get, we make a living. From what we give, we make a life.

Profit
Sales without profit is like eating soup with a fork.

Paid
You will never get paid what you are worth until you are worth more than you are paid.

Turkey
How do you keep a turkey in suspense? I'll tell you tomorrow.

Laugh
Take time to laugh, it is the music of the soul. We do not laugh because we are happy. We are happy because we laugh.

I Never
When I started selling CUTCO 60 years ago, I was only going to do it until I found something better. I never did find anything better.
Life without CUTCO — I DON'T THINK SO.

What Do You Do, Jerry?
When someone asked me what I do for a living, I would reply, "I am a builder. I build people."

Why?
One day, Don Lund asked me why I always answer a question with a question. I replied, "Do I?"

My South Dakota Pheasant Hunting Story
I won a six-day South Dakota Pheasant Hunting Contest. Afterwards, I had to win the right to sleep on a bed versus the floor and not to have to cook.

We hunted pheasants all day and played cards all night. It was my job to scare up the pheasants while the other CUTCO division manager shot the pheasants. It was a wonderful trip.

Ray Deardorff, our region manager from Minneapolis, slept in a sleeping bag on the floor. One night a mouse got into his sleeping bag while he was sleeping. That is when Mr. Deardorff said that the mouse knew more about him than anyone except for his wife.

Four Meetings a Year in the Big City
I would get up at 3:00 in the morning (good thing I was young) on Thursday and drive to Minneapolis for a CUTCO division managers meeting that started at 1:00 p.m. The meeting was held from 1:00-6:00 p.m., dinner was from 6:00-7:30 p.m. and then from 7:30 p.m. until 7:00 the next morning we played the card game 7 ½. We would not get any sleep. We would have breakfast and meet on Friday from 9:00 a.m. until 6:00 p.m. We then had din-

ner and played cards until 7:00 a.m. on Saturday morning. Again we would get no sleep. On Saturday our meeting lasted from 9:00 a.m. to 1:00 p.m. and then I would drive home. I slept for over a day when I got home. We all liked and respected each other and laughed all the time. Most people do not laugh enough. <u>Laugh a lot and you will live longer.</u>

The Secret
The secret of success is WORK.

Are You Rich?
Rich is a state of mind. If you are happy, you are rich. If people really like and love you, you are rich. If you help people do better, you are rich. If you are kind, you are rich. Are you rich?

Words of Wisdom
Success is peace of mind. Joy is knowing you helped as many people as possible. Years wrinkle the skin but when you give up enthusiasm, it wrinkles the soul.

Enthusiasm
You can do anything if you have enthusiasm. Enthusiasm is the yeast that makes your hopes rise to the stars. Enthusiasm is the sparkle in your eye, it is the swing in your gait, the grip of your hand, the irresistible surge of your will and your energy to execute your ideas. Enthusiasts are fighters. They have fortitude. They have staying qualities. Enthusiasm is at the bottom of all progress – with it there is accomplishments, without it there are only alibis.

Worry
Worry is like a rocking chair. It gives you something to do but it does not get you anywhere. I have never worried a day of my life. I have been concerned a few times.

To Tell You the Truth
Never say, "to tell you the truth" or "honestly" because that means you are telling the truth now but you lied before and will lie again. Always tell the truth and you do not have to remember what you said.

Business Is Great
Business is great. People are terrific. Life is wonderful. These three sentences are the most positive sentences you could tell anyone. This is an exceptional time to be alive.

My Customers
My CUTCO customers live 21 years longer than my non-customers. Well maybe 20 years longer. I have never lost a customer because I give exceptional service to them. The only customers I have lost are the ones that passed away.

That's Once
Someone said to me, "Jerry you are right." That is once in a row.

Approaching
I am approaching the prime of my life and I am only 85!

Failure
Failure is not an option.

Gerry and Pauline Degroot
Gerry and Pauline Degroot are two of my CUTCO customers. They live in Little Chute so you already know they are good people. These are real friends. Pauline makes the best pie in the world.

Delores Chizek
Delores has been a good customer and good friend for many years.

Paulette Laffin
Paulette is a good friend of mine from Rotary. She has a great husband Emory. Paulette is a wonderful person.

Jerry Ellefson
Donna and me knew Jerry and Marge Ellefson from Trinity Lutheran Church in Appleton. Jerry had a wonderful voice and he sang a solo, *Amazing Grace,* which was fantastic. Before I got fat, some said that Jerry and I looked alike. After church, a lady said to me, "You sang very well." I said, "Thanks." If he had sung it poorly, I would have said it was Jerry Ellefson singing.

Pat Lewis
Pat is one of my true friends that takes me on errands often. He also has a wonderful wife. He married up.

Erick J. Laine
Erick is the majority owner of Cutco. When he enters a room, he changes it. <u>We are all very proud of Erick Laine.</u>

Frank Rippl
Frank plays the piano at the Rotary Club of Appleton. Frank is a great musician and all the members of the Club are very proud of him. Vince Lombardi liked Frank and so does everyone that knows him.

Many Sales Managers Do Not
Many managers with our company and other companies do not recognize "red flags," or problems, soon enough. By the time they recognize a red flag it is too late.

Married Up
Most great managers with CUTCO that are married, married up. <u>A man is only as good as his wife. It is nice to be married to the right wife, which I did twice.</u>

Interview
When I interviewed anyone to be a manager and they were engaged or married, I would insist that the fiancé or wife/husband come as well.

You Have to Be Tough
Many years ago, I was in a car accident on my way to a CUTCO division meeting. I was thrown out of the car. I landed on my head and was knocked out. Since the car was okay, we drove to our meeting in Green Bay. We arrived just barely on time. Except for that day, I always arrived at the division meetings one-and-a-half to two hours early.

When I got back to Appleton, I went to the hospital. The doctor said to me, "Jerry, you must be tough since you are okay." It's a good thing I'm Norwegian. Our daughter Toni thinks I'm a medical miracle. I am tougher than nails.

Average
Never be average because average is the lousiest of the best or the best of the lousiest. Do not be average.

Pretty Good
"There once was a pretty good student, who
sat in a pretty good class,
And was taught by a pretty good teacher,
who always let pretty good pass.
He was terrific at reading, he wasn't a whiz-bang at math,
But for him, education was leading
straight down a pretty good path.
He didn't find school too exciting, but he wanted to do pretty well,
And he did have some trouble with writing,
and nobody had taught him to spell.
When doing arithmetic problems,
pretty good was regarded as fine.
Five plus five didn't always add up to 10;
a pretty good answer was nine.
The pretty good class that he sat in
was part of a pretty good school.
And the student was not an exception;
on the contrary, he was the rule.
The pretty good school that he went to
was there in a pretty good town.
And nobody there seemed to notice he
could not tell a verb from a noun.
The pretty good student, in fact, was part of a pretty good mob.
And the first time he knew what he lacked
was when he looked for a pretty good job.
It was then, when he sought a position,
he discovered that life could be tough.
And he soon had a sneaky suspicion pretty good
might not be good enough.
The pretty good town in our story was part of a pretty good state,
Which had pretty good aspirations and paid for a pretty good fate.
There once was a pretty good nation,
pretty proud of the greatness it had,

Which learned much too late, if you want to be great,
pretty good is, in fact, pretty bad".

You Can Become
You can become twice as good at something you are already good at faster than you can cut a weakness in half. In other words, it is easier to grow the talents you possess because you have momentum.

Talking to Myself
I talk to myself sometimes. Is this a good thing? In my case, I think it is because I don't get any back talk, I always agree with myself and I am always right.

Please
Before you give a talk and you are going to tell some jokes, and only a few laugh, say "Please laugh as a group. If you laugh individually, we will never get out of here."

Your Next Talk
Do not tell any jokes in your talk unless you are good at it.

The Funnier They Will Be
By telling Norwegian jokes in your talk, tell your audience that the more you laugh the funnier they will be. So you see, it is all up to you!

Sales
If you are in sales, tell yourself every morning, "Self, have a great week today." We used to say this to every sales representative. It is very positive and simple. We are what we think about most of the time. Have a will-do attitude. No matter how good you are now, you can always be better. Always give people a mental pat on the back. Walk on the sunny side of the street. Learn to like people and look for the best in them.

Just for Me
If the audience does not laugh at some of Jerry Otteson's jokes say, "Some of these jokes are just for me!"

Product Conviction

If you have enough product conviction, you cannot use high pressure even if you try.

Gem of the Day

For people who want to succeed in life, I strongly recommend some four-letter words: work, risk, guts and zest.

Public Speaking

If you want to be a great public speaker, do not say, "you know," "ah" or "okay" every other word. If you do, people will start counting how many times you say them per minute. These are all fillers or pauses. If you say nothing at these pauses, you will be a much better speaker.

Mirror Test

Before you give a sales demonstration of a product or service, do it in front of a mirror and tape it. When you do this you will know exactly how you look and sound to your customer. You will see many mistakes no matter how good you are. Remember to take the mirror test.

Words That Work

Just do it. Get' er done. Life is good. We have nothing to fear but fear itself.

Consistency, Thou Art a Jewel

The CUTCO dairyland division (Wisconsin and Upper Michigan) and our North Dakota division were in the top 10 divisions in the United States 19 out of 27 years. It is because we had wonderful managers and sales representatives and we field-trained more and better than most divisions. We also did personal recruiting better and more consistently than the rest. We worked as a team. Remember there is no "I" in team.

Donna and I won a trip to Nice, France. Win every sales contest and you will succeed. You are not selling CUTCO, you are selling yourself. If people like you, they will probably invest in what you are selling. If they do not like you, they will not purchase your product. It is that simple.

Donna, A. P. Miller and me in Nice, France during a Cutco trip

Bruce Goodman

Bruce is the president of the western half of the United States for Cutco and is doing a wonderful job. Keep up the good work, Bruce. <u>You are a good man, Bruce.</u>

Curt Holub

If Curt Holub had stayed with our great company instead of becoming a minister, he would have been a Regional Manager.

Curt used to write out six postcards before he left for CUTCO demos. He had the same message on each card, "Thanks for your CUTCO order. I appreciate your business. If you ever have a question, call me." Before he went home that night, he addressed one postcard to each person he sold to that day and mailed them. One day, a customer invested in only a trimmer but Curt still sent the postcard. The next morning the customer called Curt and said, "I buy a Caddy every year and I never got a postcard." She then ordered a complete set of CUTCO.

Curt's customers still remember his name even 40 years after they invested in CUTCO from him. Will your customers remember your name 40 years from now?

Worst CUTCO Training

The worst field training was the one done for Marty Domitrovich. Marty was a personal recruit of Clare Wilman's. Field training is when a new CUTCO recruit goes with another sales representative and watches him/her give demonstrations. Clare was going to field train Marty. He had only one appointment for Saturday morning at 9:00 but he picked up Marty at noon. Of course, the 9:00 appointment was not at home since they were three hours late. Clare then took Marty to the lobby at the dorm and gave him a CUTCO demonstration. People walked by and made fun of Marty and Clare. Marty hitchhiked home to Ontonagon, Michigan and sold Saturday night and Sunday then went back to college on Sunday night. At the time Marty was only 18 years old. I took over Marty's training.

Listening

The only time that Marty did not listen to me is when he and Clare decided to drive from Ontonagon, Michigan to Detroit, Michigan to sell CUTCO cutlery. They sold nothing and almost starved to death. This is a perfect example of making our own problems. With their last dollar, they bought a bag of apples. Neither Marty nor Clare dared to go to sleep in the car because they were afraid the other would eat all the apples. They finally sold a CUTCO Deluxe Carving set. Now they had enough money to buy gas so they could drive home. Marty learned a lot that day. We remember when we make a mistake that costs us money.

Caddy Versus Chevy Story

Marty was a student at Northland College in Ashland, Wisconsin. Marty, his wife Karen and their daughter DeeDee (for double D grind) lived in Ashland. I was scheduled to drive to Ashland in two days to work with Marty and his CUTCO team. He called me and said that he wanted to buy a new car when I was there. He asked me if he should buy a Chevy or a Cadillac. I told him to buy a Cadillac, of course. When I arrived in Ashland, we went to the Cadillac dealer. Forty-five minutes later, Marty bought a Cadillac and the owner of the dealership bought all the CUTCO we had at the time.

I Have Never Been So Proud

People ask me what I am the most proud of in my 60 years in the wonderful world of CUTCO. I am the most proud of developing Marty. He set one record that will never be broken. He developed seven Cutco region managers and there are only six region managers today and 27 division managers and hundreds of district managers. Every other record in our company's history will be broken except this one. I am not sure there would be a company without Marty. Marty D. managed like I did, but much, much, much better!

Respect

I knew a manager that always said, "I do not care if they like me as long as they respect me." I always wondered why we couldn't have both. Every great CUTCO manager I have ever known had both. We all earn respect.

Self-Made Man

Marty Domitrovich was a self-made man. A self-made person has many working parts. His father and mother were born in Croatia, Yugoslavia. His father reminded me of my own father: great work ethic, good sense of humor, likeable and very little education but a lot of common sense. Common sense is not very common anymore. Marty's father and mother wanted to pay Marty's college expenses but Marty wanted to pay them all himself. I was very impressed by this.

Have You Noticed?

Have you ever noticed that if you have a week to do a job that it takes a week? If you have a day to do a job, it takes a day. If you have an hour to do a job it will take an hour. Isn't that interesting?

Good Things

Most of the good things that have happened to me in my life happened because I did something I should have done and I didn't do something that I shouldn't have done. Most of the bad things that happened to me in my life were because I did something I should not have done or did not do something I should have done. It's that simple. I do not believe in luck. We make our own luck 99% of the time. Remember the things that make you glad and forget the things that make you sad. If you ask me to remember some sad thing in my life, I can't remember it — on purpose. Life is not fair — get used to it.

The Importance of Consistency
During the 60 years that I have been with CUTCO, I was never the number one sales representative for the week but I always had a good week. Why be consistent in sales? Otherwise you sell $3,000 one week, a paring knife the next and then some went out of business the third. If you are not consistent, you will have chicken one night for dinner then feathers the next. The best predictor of the future is the past.

Listing
If you are listing a group of names from a podium, always have the list in front of you. Otherwise no matter how young or how smart you are you will forget someone's name, which is not good.

Which Do You Do?
Some people brighten up a room by entering it. Some people brighten up a room by leaving it. Which do you do?

Favorite Sayings
Mark Twain said that any three people can keep a secret if two of them are dead.

Age is mind over matter. If you do not mind, it does not matter.

If your memory starts to fail, forget it. I do this many times a day.

When you get to know me, you will like me. I know this because I already like you.

I am not handy around the house. The other day, I cut myself on the plunger.

Doris is my favorite sister. Doris tells everyone that she is my ONLY sister. That is true but she is still my favorite.

You are not born a winner or a loser. You are born a chooser.

Winners vs. Losers

"The winner is always a part of the answer."
The loser is always a part of the problem.
The winner always has a program.
The loser always has an excuse.
The winner says, "Let me do it for you."
The loser says, "That's not my job."
The winner sees an answer for every problem.
The loser sees a problem in every answer.
The winner sees a green near every sand trap.
The loser sees two or three sand traps near every green.
The winner says, "It may be difficult, but it's possible."
The loser says, "It may be possible, but it's too difficult."

If It Is to Be, It Is Up to Me

Winners are not passionate because they are successful;
they are successful because they are passionate.
Be an action person. Don't wait to get motivated before you do
something.
Do something and you'll get motivated.
What you conceive in your mind and believe in your heart,
you will achieve.
Nothing positive will come from being negative, and
Nothing negative will come from being positive.
Winners look for ways things can be done;
losers look for reasons they can't.
In order to be a real champion, you have to believe in yourself
when no one else will.
Don't mistake activity for achievement.
Just because you're moving fast doesn't mean you're
going somewhere.
Losers visualize the penalties of failure;
winners visualize the rewards of success.
Things work out best for those who make the best
out of the way things work out.
Finally, ask yourself the following question:
If you were on trial for living the life of a winner,
Would the jury have enough evidence to convict you?
If you shoot for the moon and miss, at least you'll be one of the
stars.

49

Best CUTCO Field Training Story

I was field training a sales representative in Appleton, Wisconsin. I had the perfect prospect. She lived with her mother (her father had passed away), didn't pay rent and was engaged to be married in a year. She (as well as her fiancé) had great full-and part-time jobs. We had an appointment with a perfect prospect. When we got to the house, the mother came to the door. I had never met her mother before. She answered the door and said, "<u>She is not interested</u>" and slammed the door in my face, almost breaking my nose. I went to the other door of the same house and the same mother came to the door and I said, "<u>I hope you are not related to the lady that came to the other door because did she ever give me a bad time.</u>"

The mother laughed so hard she almost fell on the floor. She said, "Oh, come on in." The mother and daughter bought all the CUTCO we made at the time. The CUTCO reference names they gave me invested in over $10,000. Thirty-five years ago, $10,000 in personal sales was a lot.

The Start of Something Big

In 1968, CUTCO managers Marty Domitrovich, Ken Schmidt, Denny Mahoney, Jeff Meyer and I drove 2,000 miles to Olean, New York and back for a meeting. We talked about many things but the most important thing we discussed was what would happen if we interviewed 10, 20, 30, 40 or even 50 people at one time and then individually afterwards instead of one, two or three like the company had been doing for years.

We made many mistakes but we got a lot of business. The second summer we did better and the third we did great. We hired a big Hertz truck to issue CUTCO samples to all that had been at this seminar. <u>We had $56,676 for the first push week. This was by far the most any CUTCO Division had ever had for a push week in the history of our company at that time. Some managers have forgotten how to teach</u>.

CUTCO Son #3

Denny Mahoney is my CUTCO son #3. He probably saved more people from leaving our great business than anyone else. When someone was thinking of leaving our company, we sent them with Denny on sales calls. They ended up staying with our company. Denny's wife Mary is great.

Laying the groundwork for the record-breaking week, division manager Jerry Otteson and field counselor Kenneth Schmidt wind up the training seminar for some of the enthusiastic new distributors recently contracted.

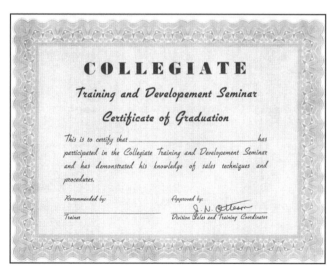

We gave this certificate to everyone that graduated from our third year seminar. $56,626 for the week!

Issuing CUTCO samples from a Hertz truck after training

CUTCO NATIONAL SALES REPORT

Week Ending June 19, 1970

RECORD SMASHING WEEK BY CHICAGO REGION

(See Inside for 3 Star Extra)

TOP TEN DISTRIBUTORS

Name	Region	Amount
J. Carr	Clev.	$ 2,631
G. DeLaitsch	Chi.	2,207
K. Kratz	Chi.	2,184
J. Cigelske	Chi.	1,667
D. Gerber	Chi.	1,661
D. Mahoney	Chi.	1,644
D. Hannah	N. Y.	1,544
F. Fenzl	Chi.	1,525
J. Winter	N. Y.	1,515
S. Keithly	S. F.	1,460

TOP TEN COUNSELORS

Name	Region	Amount
R. Fenzl	Chi.	$ 8,665
P. Beisel	Chi.	7,326
T. Kent	Chi.	5,969
C. Kobayashi	S. F.	4,866
T. Massey	Chi.	4,360
P. Connolly	Atl.	3,761
R. VanOosterhout	Clev.	3,458
D. Shawgo	Chi.	3,182
J. Mallon	Chi.	3,112
C. Zanna	N. Y.	3,080

TOP TEN FIELD COUNSELORS

Name	Region	Amount
J. Meyer	Chi.	$20,511
M. Domitrovich	Chi.	14,100
K. Schmidt	Chi.	9,809
D. Mahoney	Chi.	9,176
M. Avecilla	S. F.	8,075
G. Mahaffey	K. C.	6,835
P. Bailey	N. Y.	6,803
W. Smith	K. C.	6,317
J. Horst	Atl.	5,935
R. Herrold	Clev.	5,927

SALES BY REGIONS

First	Second
B. W. BREKKEN Chicago	V. W. BRANCATO New York

Region	Sales Opps.	No. Sales	$ per Call	Amount
Chicago	2,562	1,160	40	$102,814
New York	1,658	833	36	60,473
Cleveland	1,250	503	31	39,303
San Francisco	952	413	37	35,291
Kansas City	1,252	520	21	26,736
Atlanta	1,018	517	24	24,052
TOTALS	8,692	3,946	33	$288,669

TOP TEN DIVISIONS

First	Second
J. OTTESON Chicago	R. JIGUERE New York

Name	Region	Amount
J. Otteson	Chi.	$56,676
R. Jiguere	N. Y.	19,141
A. DeCaprio	N. Y.	16,615
J. Vaughn	Atl.	14,895
J. Miller	Chi.	14,294
J. Hedbor	K. C.	12,331
J. Ozzello	Chi.	10,932
L. Hansen	Chi.	10,315
E. Krizin	Clev.	9,348
D. Mahoney	Chi.	9,176

Our CUTCO division had about 19% of all of the United States put together. $56,626 in this 7-day push week. Wow!

Ken Schmidt, Tom Koehler and Terry Kent

Ken Schmidt, Tom Koehler and Terry Kent each invested in new Corvettes while they were going to business school in Milwaukee. They also paid for all their college expenses by selling CUTCO. Only in America. Ken is my #2 Cutco son.

Nine Great Rules

One — Never wrestle with a pig; you both get dirty and the pig likes it.

Two - Never argue with an idiot; people watching may not be able to tell the difference.

Three- Observe everything.

Four - It's easier to obtain forgiveness than it is permission.

Five - Rarely resist the opportunity to keep your mouth shut.

Six- If you want a new idea, read an old book.

Seven - If you don't know where you're going, any road will get you there.

Eight - Never have a philosophy which supports a lack of courage.

Nine - Never look back unless you intend to go that way.

Biggest Sports

One of the biggest sports in the world is feeling sorry for yourself. Never attend a pity party.

United States of China

One of my customers thought we lived in the United States of China. I laughed out loud. Sometimes we laugh when we should be crying. World-famous CUTCO knives are made in the good old United States, not some foreign country.

Value

Until you value yourself, you won't value your time. Until you value your time, you will not do anything with it. Be somebody and do something!

You Can't

You can't keep the birds of prey of negative thinking from flying over your head. You can keep them from building a nest on it. Develop a **can do** attitude.

Press On

Nothing in the world can take the place of persistence. Talent will not; nothing is more common than unsuccessful men and women with talent. Genius will not; unrewarded genius is almost a proverb. Education will not; the world is full of educated derelicts. Persistence and determination alone are important.

First CUTCO (Wearever) Hall of Fame

I won the first CUTCO (Wearever) Hall of Fame ring. The year was 1970 and our great company had their first Hall of Fame at their home office. Jack Hamilton was the president of our company at the time. The five winners were: Tony DeCaprio, division manager; Jerry Otteson, division manager; Mercedes Dunn Sacks, personal sales; Patty Reynolds, personal sales; and Rodella Cortez, counselor. We are charter Hall of Fame winners.

1998 CUTCO Hall of Fame

My wife Donna and I received the Honorary CUTCO Hall of Fame award in Banff, Canada. This is the biggest honor I have ever received in my 60 years with CUTCO.

Donna and Jerry (1998 CUTCO Hall of Fame)

The Otto Cup
This is an excerpt from a weekly central region mailing.

The Otto Cup is similar to the All-American race, except that it is for non-student reps. This contest pits the best in the central region against top reps from across the nation.

Like the All-American race, the Otto Cup is a national competition. Those central region reps that finish any of Vector's three campaigns in the National Top 25 will be awarded a beautiful silver Otto Cup and a letter of recommendation.

This competitive race is named for Jerry Otteson, one of the all-time legends in the CUTCO business and a member of the central region team. Jerry is definitely one of the great salesmen in our company with two million dollars retail sold during a career which has spanned over 60 years.

By taking full advantage of the Vector Opportunity, and working a disciplined schedule, you can not only prove yourself to be one of the best in the central region, you can also have this prestigious award to display in your home or office.

Hi, Chet
We did business with the 1st National Bank in Appleton for years. I went to the bank three or four times a week and this man that worked in the bank always said to me, "Good morning, Chet." I said, "It's Jerry," but he kept calling me Chet. I said to myself, "I have been called worse," so I stopped correcting him.

If you call someone by the wrong name, your chance of continuing to call them by the wrong name goes up dramatically.

Vegetarian
I could very easily be a vegetarian if I could eat meat twice a day.

Do Not
Do not get the big head. Marty Domitrovich was still just as down-to-earth as when he first started working for CUTCO at the age of 18. Many sales managers are ruined because they got the big

head. They never develop anyone else that was any good because they also get a big head.

My Customers
Ken and Barb Kleczka have been wonderful CUTCO customers of mine for a long time. They were at Donna's funeral and I am very grateful for that.

Vince Lombardi
I have read all the books about Vince Lombardi. Some of the highlights include:

- Winning is a habit; unfortunately, so is losing.
- If you could have won, you should have won.
- You do not do things right once in a while, you do them right all the time.
- There is no laughter in losing.
- If winning was not important, they would not keep score.
- If you do not think you are a winner, you do not belong here.

Two Great Salesmen: John Wooden and Al McGuire
John Wooden is the greatest college basketball coach that ever lived. He won 10 national titles in 12 years at UCLA. This record will never be broken.

Al McGuire was the basketball coach at Marquette University in Milwaukee, Wisconsin. His team was in the top 10 in the USA 10 years in a row. The best college basketball game I ever saw was when Marquette won the National Championship in 1977. They should have not been in the playoffs but they were and they won.

I have read all the books that Al McGuire wrote and all the books written about him. Some of the highlights include:

- Some of the things Al said about his assistant Hank Raymond, such as "Hank is a perfectionist. If he married Dolly Parton, he'd expect her to cook."
- It is a mortal sin to not live up to your potential.
- You do not give excuses, and you do not take excuses.

- I never intentionally hurt anyone.
- Nothing else matters when they will run through a wall for you.
- Al made his players mentally tough.
- Do not waste your time with N.C. (no chance) players.

Al said he was a chain recruiter. After the first two years, he had his players recruiting for him. We call this personal recruiting in our company.

"C" Students

Al McGuire said that "C" students ran the world. I told this to my Rotary friend, Tom Scullen, Superintendent of the Appleton Area School District, and he said, "Maybe B's." Tom was a great man, a wonderful superintendent and he had many friends.

Too Long

When you start your demo, you should tell the customer that you are far behind showing CUTCO and if it is all right with them, you will hurry. The customer will be thrilled because they are concerned about you being there too long. This will save you at least 20 minutes on every demo and the customer will like it. If the customer gets off on a tangent, tell them to remember that we have to hurry. <u>Most demos are too long</u>.

Life

Life is wonderful. It always has been and it always will be. Enthusiasm is contagious; let's start an epidemic.

The Final Analysis

People are often unreasonable, illogical, and self-centered.
Forgive them anyway.
If you are kind, people may accuse you of selfish ulterior motives.
Be kind anyway.
If you are successful, you will win some false friends and some enemies. Succeed anyway.
If you are honest and frank, people may cheat you.
Be honest and frank anyway.
What you spend years building, some may destroy overnight.

Build anyway.
If you find serenity and happiness, they may be jealous.
Be happy anyway.
The good you do today, people will often forget tomorrow.
Do well anyway.
Give the world the best you have and it may never be enough.
Give the world the best you have anyway.
You see, in the final analysis, it's all between you and God.
It was never between you and them anyway.

Today
This is the beginning of a new day.
I can waste it or use it for good.

What I do today is important because
I am exchanging a day of my life for it.

When tomorrow comes, this day will be gone forever,
leaving in its place something I have traded for it.

I want it to be gain, I want it to be good,
I want it to be success, I want it to be prosperity;
In order that I shall not regret the price I paid for today!

One of the Great Poems
Tomorrow's not so far away.
Nor is the goal you seek.
Today you should be training
For the work you'll do next week.
The bigger job is just ahead,
Each day new changes bring.
Suppose that post were vacant now.
Could you take charge of things?
It is not enough to know enough
To do your job today.
It's not enough to do enough
To earn your weekly pay.
Someday there will be a vacancy with greater things to do.
Will you be ready for that job,
When it shall fall to you?

Be ready!

The Dash
I've seen my share of tombstones, but never took the time to truly read,
The meaning behind what is there for others to see.

Under the person's name it read the date of birth,
dash (-), and the date the person passed.
But the more I think about that tombstone, the important thing is
the dash.

Yes, I see the name of the person but that I might forget,
I also read the date of birth and death but even that might not stick.

But thinking about the individual, I can't help to remember **the dash**,
Because it represents a person's life and that will always last.

So when you begin to charter your life,
make sure you're on a positive path.
Because people may forget your birth and death,
but <u>they will never forget **your dash**</u>.

Every Day
<u>Every day I break my previous record of consecutive days I have stayed alive.</u>

Four Most Important Words
If you are a manager of people, the most important four words in the world are "<u>I believe in you</u>." It is not how many times you get knocked down that counts; it is how many times you get up after you have been knocked down.

One Thousand Dollars a Week
<u>If you think $1,000 in personal sales today is a good week, get over it.</u> A $1,000 week in personal sales today is better than, better than, better than . . . it must be better than something. It is better than getting hit by a truck. That is the only thing it is better than. It is not worth writing to your mother about it. CUTCO is a $1,000-a-

day business. A $1,000 day is a good day. A $2,000 day is a very good day. A $3,000 day is a great day. Get the idea?

Lena Olson
Lena Olson, Norwegian of course, was 104 years old. Someone asked her what the advantage was to being 104 years old. Lena said, "There is no peer pressure."

Fast
Time does go fast. It goes faster than an extra large pizza at a Weight Watchers convention. Now that is fast. I am so fast that I play tennis by myself.

If
If you are planted in concrete, you are not going to grow. If you look for the good in people, you will find it. If you look for the bad in people you will also find it. If you want to be great in life, learn the power of encouragement. Sometimes the difference between giving up and going on is encouragement. Put courage into those that are discouraged.

What Are Other People Doing?
People ask me what the other people are doing now who started selling CUTCO when I did. I say, "How do I know? Most of them are dead." And most of them are dead.

Everywhere I Go
Everywhere I go today, I will overcome. Stop worrying! Just keep on keeping on. I did and I strongly recommend it. Never give up.

Do Not Worry
Do not worry! Over 70% of the things we worry about never happen.

Contact Time
Contact time is the amount of time we actually invest in front of a customer. It is usually not the best salesperson that sells the most. It is the one that makes the most demos to prospects, not suspects. If you are the best salesperson in the United States and make twelve demos a week, you are not nearly as good as the

person that makes twenty-four demos a week. When we recruit college students and high school graduates into the wonderful world of CUTCO, we suggest that they call on their friends. New CUTCO sales reps will sell more CUTCO to someone they know than someone they do not know. I get so excited selling CUTCO that my goose pimples have goose pimples. You can't be anymore excited than that.

Always Right
Store manager: I saw you were arguing with a customer who just left. I told you before that the customer is always right. Do you understand me?
Lena: Yes, sir. The customer is alvays right.
Store Manager: That's better. Now what were you arguing about?
Lena: Vell, sir. He said you ver an adiot.

Museum
Visiting the modern art museum, Lena turned to an attendant standing nearby. "Dis," she said, "I spose is one of dose hideous representations you call modern art?" "No, madam," replied the attendant. "That one's called a mirror."

Three Prisoners
Ole, Lars and Sven are three prisoners who are captured in the war, and are about to be executed. They are asked what they wish to have for their last meal. Lars asks for pepperoni pizza, which he is served and then taken away. Sven requests a filet mignon, which he is served and then taken away. Ole requests a lot of strawberries. The captors are surprised and reply, 'STRAW-BERRIES?' "Yes, Strawberries." 'But they are out of season!' "I can vait," said Ole.

Cracker
Ole ain't the sharpest cheese on da cracker.

Norwegian Jokes
What did the Norwegian name his pet zebra? Spot

How does a Norwegian spell farm? EIEIO

I have to admit that Norwegians are a little different. I found out just yesterday that <u>they color their eggs white</u>.

Dream Home
Ole and Lena had finally built their dream home, but the contractor had a concern: the placement of an atrium window for the walk-in shower. "I'm afraid your neighbors might have a good view of you in the nude," he said. Lena put him at ease, "Don't vorry," she said. "Dey'll only look vunce."

Nurse
Sven was in the hospital for only three days when he took a turn for the <u>nurse</u>.

Auto Repair Shop
Lena went to the auto repair shop one day and told the mechanic, "I need to get my horn fixed, because my brakes don't vork."

Secret
Ole with a nagging secret couldn't keep it any longer. In the confessional, he admitted that for years he had been stealing building supplies from the lumberyard where he worked.

"What did you take?" his priest asked.

"Enuf to build my own house and enough fer my son's house. And houses fer our two daughters and our cottage at da lake.

"This is very serious," the priest said. "I shall have to think of a far-reaching penance. Have you ever done a retreat?"

"No, Fadder, I hafen't," Ole replied. "But if you can get da plans, I can get da lumber."

Party
Ole and Lena were returning from a party one evening. As the couple was driving home, she asked Ole, "Honey, has anyone efer told you how handsome,, sexy and irresistible to vomen you are?" Totally flattered, Ole replied, "No, dear they hafen't." At that point she yelled, "den vhat da heck gave you DAT idea at da party tonight?"

Credit
Lena's credit is so bad that they will not even take her cash.

Peach Pie
Lena: The only 2 things I can make is peach pie and meatballs.
Ole: Which one is this?

Childhood Memories
Knute: What kinda childhood memories do ya have?
Ole: Vell, let me tink .. oh ya .. until I vas 14 I thought my
name was SHUT UP!

Cemetery
Ole said that his luck was so bad that if he bought a cemetery
people would stop dying.

Moving Furniture
Co-workers sympathized as Lena complained that her back
was really sore from moving furniture. "Vhy don't you vait till
yer husband gets home?" Tina asked. "I could," Lena told the
group, "but da couch is easier to move if he's not on it."

Statue
Ole said, "Sven, you are slower than a statue."

What's Your Name
Ole asked Sven, "What's your name?" Ole said, "How soon do
you need to know?"

Good Time
Ole said, "I am lost, but I am making very good time."

Bad Turn Off
"Ole, do not move. I want to forget you just the way you are."

Dinner
Ole was sitting on the sofa watching TV when he heard Lena's
voice from the kitchen. "Vhat would you like for dinner, honey?
Shicken, beef or lamb?" Ole said, "Tank you, I'll have shicken."
"Shut up. You're having soup. I was talking to the cat."

Half Drunk
Ole comes home from a night of drinking with the boys. As he falls through the doorway of his house, Lena snaps at him, "Vhat's the big idea coming home half drunk?" Ole replies, "I'm sorry, Lena. <u>I ran out of money.</u>"

Fence
When Ole was building a fence he worked very, very fast. When Sven asked him what the hurry was, Ole replied, "I vant to get done before I run outta nails."

Ole Said
"We were so poor that when all the other kids had sleds, I had to coast down the hill on my cousin."

Grandfather
Ole says, "When my grandfather was born, they passed out cigars. When my father was born, they passed out cigarettes. When I was born, they just passed out."

Burglar
Ole went to the police station wishing to speak with the burglar who had broken into his house the night before. "You'll get your chance in court," said the desk sergeant. "No, no, no!" said Ole. "I vant to know how he got into da house vithout vaking Lena. I've been trying to do dat fer jears!"

First Day of College
On the first day of college, the dean addressed the students, pointing out some of the rules:
- The female dormitory will be out of bounds for all male students, and the male dormitory to the female students.
- Anybody caught breaking this rule will be fined $20 the first time.
- Anybody caught breaking this rule the second time will be fined $60.
- Being caught a third time will cost you $180.

Are there any questions? <u>"How much for a season pass?"</u> asked Ole.

Routine Physical

Ole goes to a doctor for a routine physical. The nurse starts with the basics. "How much do you weigh?" she asked.

"Oh, about one sixty-five," he says.

The nurse puts him on he scale. It turns out that his weight is 187. The nurse asks, "Your height?"

"Oh, about six feet," he says.

The nurse checks and sees that he's only 5 feet 8 ¾ inches. She then takes his blood pressure, and it's very high.

"High!", Ole explains. "Well, Vhat did you expect? Vhen I came in here, I vas tall and lanky. Now, I'm short and fat!"

Bottle of Viskey

Ole walked into a bar crying. One of the other men in the bar asked him what happened. "I did a terrible thing," sniffed the drunk, "Yust a few hours ago I sold Lena to somevun for a bottle of vhiskey."

"That is awful," said the other guy, "And now that she is gone you want her back right?"

"Right!" said Ole still crying.

"You're sorry you sold her because you realized, too late, that you still loved her, right?"

"Oh, no," said Ole. "I vant her back becoss I'm tirsty again!"

I Never Get Mad

Ole: I never get mad ven I play golf. If I miss a shot I yust laugh. Yesterday, I laughed 115 times.

If I Did

Lena: How come ya can't effer agree vit me?
Ole: Vell, if I did, den ve'd both be wrong!

Ole Said
Ole said, "I am good at two things: reading, arithmetic and spelling!"

Senior Moment
Ole said, "I just had a senior moment but sometimes it lasts all day."

I Dare You to Read This in Norwegian
Saville dar deygo
A tousan busis inarow
Nojo demsnot busis dems truks
Summit cousin summit duks.

How Do You?
How do you get a one-armed Norwegian to come down out of a tree? You wave at him.

Next Week
Ole: It is our anniversary next week. Vhat do you vant for your anniversary?
Lena: I want a divorce.
Ole: I did not plan on spending that much.

Reporter
An inquiring reporter asked Lena one day: What do you think of Red China?
Lena: If you haf a vhite table cloth, it should look all right.

Average Share of Intelligence
"You seem to have an average share of intelligence for a man of your background," sneered the lawyer at a Ole on the witness stand. "If I vasn't under oath, I'd return da compliment," replied Ole.

Leg
Doctor: Your leg is swollen, but I wouldn't worry about it.
Patient: If your leg was swollen, I wouldn't worry about it either.

Oslo

Did you hear about the American who went to Oslo and met Ole? "Are you Swedish?" asked the American. "No", replied Ole, "I am Norwegian." "You look Swedish," said the American. "Vell," said Ole, "I've been sick for a couple of veeks."

First Love

Lena: Ole tell me da trut. Who vas your first love?
Ole: It vas my second grade teacher, but it didn't vork out. I vas 12 years older den her.

Pastors

Reverend Ole is the pastor of the local Norwegian Lutheran Church, and Pastor Sven is the minister of the Swedish Covenant Church across the road. One day, they were pounding a sign into the ground that read:

Da End Iss Near!
Turn Yerself Arount Now
Befor It's Too Late!

As a car sped past them, the driver leaned out his window and yelled, "Leave me alone, you Skandihoovian religions nuts!"

From the curve they heard screeching tires and a big splash.

Rev. Ole turns to Pastor Sven and asks, "<u>Do ya tink maybe da sign should yust say,</u>"
<u>BRIDGE OUT!</u>

So Dull

Ole was so dull that if he gave a fireside chat, the fire would go out.

Long-Winded

Ole was very, very long-winded and Ole said to Sven, "To make a long story short." Sven said, "It is too late." Ole is the only Norwegian I know that talks too much.

Sleeping
One night Ole and Lena were sleeping and suddenly Lena woke up. "Ole! dere's a burglar eating da cake downstairs!" "So should I call da police or da ambulance?" said Ole.

Shaking
"Doctor, doctor, You've got to help me," Ole cried. "I just can't stop my hands shaking!" "Do you drink a lot?" asked the doctor. "Not really," replied Ole, "I spill most of it!"

Mechanical Engineers
Ole and Sven worked as mechanical engineers. As they were standing at the base of a flagpole, looking up, a young lady walked by and asked what they were doing.

"Ve're supposed to find the height of the flagpole," said Sven, "but ve don't have a ladder."

The woman took a wrench from her purse, loosened a few bolts, and laid the pole down. The she took a tape measure from her pocket, took a measurement, and announced, "Eighteen feet, six inches," and walked away.

"Ole shook his head and laughed, "Ain't that yust like a voman. Ve ask for the height and she gives us the length!"

Died
Ole had died. A wonderful funeral was in progress and the country preacher talked at length of the good traits of the deceased, what an honest man he was, and what a loving husband and kind father he was.

Finally, Lena, the widow leaned over and whispered to Little Ole, "Go up dere and take a look in da coffin and make sure dat's yer pa."

Insomnia
Ole went to the doctor complaining of insomnia. The doctor gave him an exam and found nothing physically wrong with him. "Listen," the doctor said, "if you ever expect to cure your insom-

nia, you need to stop taking your troubles to bed with you."

"Dat's true", said Ole, "but Lena refuse to sleep alone."

Baby

After Ole and Lena brought their new baby home, Lena suggested that Ole should try his hand at changing diapers.

"I'm busy Lena," he said, "I'll do da next vun."

The next time came around, and Lena asked again. Ole looked puzzled. "Oh, I didn't mean da next diaper . . . I meant da next baby!"

Cheating

Ole was angry when he found out that his Lena had been cheating on him. He shouts at her, "I vill play second fiffle to no vun!" She replied, "Second fiddle? You are lucky you are still in da band!"

Fertility Specialist

With the help of fertility specialist, a 65-year-old woman, Lena, has a baby. All her relatives come to visit and meet the newest member of their family. When they ask to see the baby, Lena says, "Not yet."

A little later they ask to see the baby again. Again Lena says, "Not yet."

Finally they say, "When can we see the baby?"

And Lena says, "<u>Vhen da baby cries.</u>"

So they ask, "Why do we have to wait until the baby cries?"

"<u>Becoss I can't remember vhere I put it.</u>" said Lena.

M&M's

Ole: Vott hass Little Ole been doin' all day?
Lena: Oh, he's been tryin' to put a bag of M&M's in alphabetical

order.

Peel
Why don't Norwegians eat M&M's? They are too hard to peel.

Light Bulb
Ingeborg: How many divorced men do ya tink it takes to change a light bulb?
Lena: Who cares? Most of em' don't get da house anyhow.

Bald
Ole: Yikes! I tink I'm goin' bald!
Lena: Don't tink of it as losing hair. Tink of it as gainin' face.

Surgery
Sven: How did yer surgery go?
Ole: Terrible. Yust before I vent under I hard da surgeon say da most awful 4-letter verd!
Sven: Oh no! Vott vas it?
Ole: He said . . . "Oops"!

Six Months to Live
Sven: Ya look real happy today, Ole!
Ole: I am. My doctor gave me 6 months to live. I couldn't pay his bill so he gave me anudder six months!

Clumsy
Lena: Ole iss so clumsy.
Ingeborg: Vott hass he done now?
Lena: He tripped over da cordless phone!

Acupuncture
Ole: I tink dere might be sumting to dis acupuncture stuff.
Lars: How didja figger dat out?
Ole: Vell, didja effer notice dat dere ain't any sick porcupines?

Parole Officer
Ole: Boy . . . I'm tellin' ya . . Lena vould've made a great parole officer.
Ingeborg: Vott makes ya say dat?
Ole: She never lets me finish a sentence!

Travels
Lena: Light travels faster dan sound. Dis is vy some folks seem smart until ya hear dem speak!

She Wasn't Even
Service in the restaurant was unusually slow. Ole was starting to flip out, so Lena tried to distract him with small talk. "Yew know," she said, "our friend Tina should be having her baby anytime now." "Really?" Ole snapped. "She vasn't even pregnant vhen ve walked in here."

Best Thing
What is the best thing to ever come out of Norway? An empty boat.

Henpecked
Ole was so henpecked, he was not even in his wedding picture.

Great Advice
Improve your image – be seen with a Norwegian.

Not Finished Yet
Lena got up one morning, looked at Ole and said, "Vhat are you going to do today?" "Nutting", he replied. "Dat's vat you did yesterday!" "Ya, but I'm not finished yet."

Mirror
Ole was standing in front of the mirror with his eyes closed. Lena asked "What you are doing?" Ole said, "I vant to see how I look vhile I am sleeping."

Mental Problem
Ole says that he married his wife Lena because of a mental problem. He vas out of his mind at the time.

Old Enough

Ole: Ya know vott I finally figgered out?

Knute: I ain't got no idea!

Ole: I'm old enough now so I know my vay around, and now all uff a sudden . . . I ain't goin' anyvere!

A Raise

"I haf to have a raise," Ole said to his boss. "Dere are tree other companies after me."

"Is that so?" asked the manager. "What other companies are after you?"

"Da electric company, da telephone company, and da gas company."

Library

Lena went to the library to get a book. A few days later, she returns and says to the librarian at the counter, "The book vas very boring. It had too many characters and too many numbers, so I vould like to return it." The librarian says to the other librarian, "So here is the person who took our phone book!"

Sermon

One Sunday, Ole thought the sermon dragged on too long, so he left church early. The next day on the street, the minister met Ole and said, "I saw you left church early yesterday. Why did you do that?"

Ole said, "I had to get a haircut," to which the minister replied, "Couldn't you have done that before church?"

Ole replied, "I didn't need it den."

Kids

Ole and Lena had been married for 45 years and had raised a brood of 11 children and was blessed with 22 grandchildren. When asked the secret for staying together all that time, Lena replied, "Many jears ago ve made a promise to each udder: da first vun to pack up and leave has to take all da kids."

You Will Remember Much More

For over 60 years whenever I talk to anyone on the phone, a friend, customer, CUTCO manager or anyone else, I take notes. Often I never look at my notes and other times I look at all my notes; but I always remember what was said on the telephone five times as much as I would have without notes.

Attitudes

Of all the "attitudes" we can acquire, surely the attitude of gratitude is the most important and by far the most life-changing.

Chickens

Ole told Sven, "If you can tell me how many chickens I have in this bag, I'll give you both of them." Sven said, "Three." Ole said, "That is right."

Figures

Lars wasn't too smart, but he managed to make a fine living buying and selling used cars. He'd buy a car for $100 and sell it for $400. Lars explained, "I ain't too good at figures, but I'm satisfied vid a 3% profit."

Always Do Right

It will gratify some and astonish the rest!

Letter

Little Ole wrote, "No mom. No fun. Your son."
Ole wrote back, "How sad. Too bad. Your Dad."

Ole Thought

Ole thought Shirley Temple was a church.

Church

Tina asked her friend, Lena, if she was planning to attend church Sunday. She just shook her head. "I hafen't gone in a long time," she said. "Besides, it's too late fer me. I've probably already broken all <u>seven </u>commandments."

Dumb

One day Lena was telling Ole a joke and he could not understand it. Finally, Lena said, "Ole, you are so dumb. If yer head vas a gas tank, da needle vould be pointing to empty."

Minneapolis

Ole went to Minneapolis to see all the sights, and he had a wonderful time. When he got home, he met his friend, Sven.

"Say Ole, how vas yer trip to Minneapolis?"

"Oh Sven, I yust had such a vunderful time for four days. But on da fifth day, I had bad luck," replied Ole. "Vell, vat happened?" asked Sven.

"Well, Sven, I vas riding an escalator in a department store when da electricity vent out, and I vas stuck on da escalator fer two and vun half hours," exclaimed Ole.

"Vell, Ole, vhy didn't yew yust valk down?" asked Sven.

"I vas going up!" snapped Ole.

Looking for My Wife

Two old guys, Ole and Sigvald are pushing their carts around Walmart when they collide. Ole says to Sigvald, "Sorry about dat. I'm looking fer my vife and I guess I vasn't paying attention to vhere I vas going." Sigvald says, "Dat's OK, it's funny, I'm looking fer my vife, too. I can't find her and I'm getting a little upset."

Ole says, "Vell, maybe I can help you find her. Vhat does she look like?"
Sigvald says, "Vell, she is 27 years old, tall, vith red hair, blue eyes, long legs, and is vearing short shorts. What does your vife look like?"

To which Ole says, "Never mind, let's look for yours."

Machines

Lars: Have you ever seen one of those machines that can tell when someone is telling a lie?
Ole: Seen vun? I married one.

Coffee Shop

Ole walks into a coffee shop and asks the waitress, "How much is da coffee?" "Coffee is three dollars," the waitress says. "How much is a refill?" Ole asks. "Free," says the waitress. "Den I'll take a refill!"

They Had Words

Ole and his wife had words but Ole did no get to say his!

Jobs

Ole was applying for a new job. "Why did you leave your last job?" "It was something my boss said." "What did he say?" 'You're fired!"

One Half

Ole said he was ½ Norwegian, ½ Danish and ½ Swedish.

Old Times

Ole and Sven were talking over old times and saying how much things had changed. "I mean," said Ole, "I caught vun of da boys kissing vun of da girls yesterday." "Oh my," said Sven. "I didn't even kiss my wife Lena, before I married her, did you?" "I can't remember. Vhat vas her maiden name?"

Funeral

Ole said to Sven, "I will come to your funeral, if you will come to mine"

Money

Ole: My vife is always asking for money. Last week she asked for $100. Yesterday, she asked me for $200. And today she vanted $300.

Sven: Vat in da vorld does she do vid it all?
Ole: I don't know. I never give her any.

Housework
Lena says that she neffer gets tired of housverk because she don't do any. She neffer buys anyting vit a handle on it.

Marry Me
Ole: Why don't you marry me? Is there someone else?

Lena: <u>There must be.</u>

The Ledder
Ole was telling Sven one day, "Last night I wrote myself a ledder. But I fergot to sign it and now I don't know who it's from."

High School Reunion
Ole and Lena were at Ole's high school reunion. As Ole looked around, he noticed the other men in their expensive suits with their bulging stomachs.

Proud of the fact that he weighed just five pounds more than he did when he was in high school – the result of trying to beat a living out of a rocky hillside farm – he said to Lena, "I'm da only guy here who can vear da same suit he gradyuated in."

Lena glanced at the prosperous crowd. "Yer da only vun here who has to."

Picture
Lena was out driving when she saw the flash of a traffic camera. She figured that her picture had been taken for speeding, even though she knew she wasn't. Just to be sure, she went around the block and passed the same spot, driving even more slowly. But again the camera flashed. Thinking this was pretty funny, she drove past even slower three more times, laughing as the camera snapped away each time while she drove by it at a snail's pace. Two weeks later, Lena got five tickets in the mail for driving without a seat belt.

Waitress

After examining the paltry tips left by a church group, Lena, the waitress, was not pleased. Looking toward one of the tables, she grumbled, "Dese people come in vith da Ten Commandments and a ten-dollar bill, and dey don't break any of dem."

Christmas Eve

Ole and Lena went to the Christmas Eve service in their church, and while the minister was barely into the sermon, the electricity in the church failed. The ushers found some candles and placed them around the sanctuary. Then the minister reentered the pulpit, shuffled his notes, and muttered, "Now, vhere vas I?" Ole, with a tired voice from the back of the church yelled out, "Right near da end!"

Remarried

Ole, age 85, lived in Minneapolis and Sven, age 85, lived in Los Angeles. Ole's wife died and Ole got remarried. Sven called Ole to congratulate Ole on his new wife. Sven asked:

- "Is she good looking?" Ole said, "No she is homely!"
- "Is she rich?" Ole said, "No she is dirt poor."
- "Is she a good cook?" Ole said, "She can't boil water."
- "Is she a good housekeeper?" Ole said, "No, she is a terrible housekeeper."

Sven said, "Why did you marry her Ole?' Ole said, "She can drive at night."

Excess Weight

"Well, Ole, what are you going to do about the excess weight you're carrying around?" the doctor asked.

"I don't understand it, Doc," Ole replied. "I yust can't seem to lose veight. I must have an overactive thyroid."

"Ole, the tests show that your thyroid is perfectly normal," replied the doctor. "If anything is overactive, it's your fork."

Fishing

Ole and Sven went fishing one day. They sat in the boat for hours and never said a word. Then Sven shuffled his legs a little, trying to work out a cramp. After two more hours, Sven shuffled his legs again. Ole looked at him and said, "Did you come to fish or to practice your dancing?"

Lost Weight
Ole was sick for three weeks and lost a lot of weight. Lars remarked that Ole was so thin that when he wore a red tie, he looked like a thermometer.

Childhood
Ole often tells about his poor childhood. "Ve vas so poor – da cat and I had to share da same sandbox. The vorst part vas vhen he tried to cover me up. Food vas so scarce, sometime all ve had vas popcorn for breakfast, vater for lunch and for supper ve vould svell up."

Airplane
Lena gets on an airplane and sits down in the first class section. The stewardess tells her she must move to coach because she doesn't have a first class ticket. Lena replies, "I'm Norvegian, I'm smart, and I have a good yob and I'm staying in first class until ve reach Norvay."

The stewardess gets the head stewardess who asks Lena to leave and she says, "I'm Norvegian, I'm smart, I have a good yob and I'm staying in first class until ve reach Norvay." The stewardess does not know what to do because they have to get the rest of the passengers seated to take off, so they get the co-pilot.

The co-pilot goes up to Lena and whispers in her ear. She immediately gets up and goes to her seat in the coach section. The head stewardess asks the pilot what he said to get her to move. The co-pilot replies, "<u>I told her the front half of the airplane wasn't going to Norway</u>."

Relatives
Ole and Lena drove down a country road for several miles, not saying a word. An earlier discussion had led to an argument and neither of them wanted to concede their position. As they passed a barnyard of mules, goats and pigs, Ole asked sarcastically, "Relatives of yers?" "Yep," Lena replied, "in-laws."

State Capitals

Ole was bragging about his knowledge of the state capitals of the United States. He announced, "Go ahead, ask me any ov da capitals. I know all ov dem." "Okay," said Sven, "Vhat is the capital of Arizona?" "Oh, that is the easiest vun of all," said Ole. "It's A."

Losing Pounds

Lena and Cora were shopping. When they started to discuss their home lives, Lena said, "Seems like all Ole and I do anymore is fight. I've been so upset I've lost 20 pounds." "Vhy don't you yust leave him den?" asked Cora. "Oh! Not yet." Lena replied, "I'd like to lose at least annuder fifteen pounds first!"

Marriage

"The trill is gone from my marriage," Ole told his friend Lars.

"Vhy not add some excitement to yer life and have an affair?" Lars suggested.

"But vhat if my vife finds out?"

"Heck, dis is a new age ve live in, Ole. Go ahead and tell her about it!"

So Ole went home and said, "Lena, I tink an affair vill bring us closer togedder."

"Forget it," said Lena. "I tried dat – it never vorked."

Colic

Ole, who lived in Bergen and Sven, who lived in Oslo, both farmers, met at the state fair.

"Tell me," asked Ole, "Vhat did you give yer mule when he had the colic?"
"Turpentine," Sven answered.

A few months after the fair, they meet up again. "Say, Sven, Vhat did you say you gave ye mule vhen he vas sick with colic?" Ole asked.

"I said I gave him turpentine to MINE and it died!"

Sven nods his head. "Dat's strange. So did mine."

Listen
Ole said, "Lena says that I never listen to her! At least I think that is what she said."

Miss Right
Ole said, "I married Miss Right. I just didn't know her first name was Always."

Mudpack
Ole was telling Lars one day about Lena. He said that she got a mudpack and looked great for two days but then the mud fell off.

Grouchy
Some people are grouchy – like there was a reward for it.

Have Not Spoken
Ole said, "I have not spoken to Lena in 18 months! I did not want to interrupt her!"

Eyesight
Ole went to see his doctor one day and said, "Doctor, every morning, vhen I get up and look in da mirror . . . I feel like trowing up. Vhat's vrong vith me?" The doctor said, "I don't know but your eyesight is perfect."

New Year's Eve
Ole was hurrying to get ready for the New Year's Eve party when all of a sudden he looked at Lena and said, "Ouch! I bumped my crasy bone!" "Vell, Lena said, "Yust part your hair on the udder side and it vill never show."

Turkey
Ole: Lena's been cooking a turkey for two and a half days. It said a half hour per pound and Lena weighs 180.

Old

Old is when your friends compliment you on your new alligator shoes and you're barefoot.

Retiree

Ole, a new retiree-greeter at WalMart, just couldn't seem to get to work on time. Every day he was 5, 10, 15 minutes late. But he was a good worker, really tidy, clean shaven , sharp minded and a real credit to the company and obviously demonstrating their "Older Person Friendly" policies.

One day the boss called him into the office for a talk.

"Ole, I have to tell you I like your work ethic, you do a bang-up job, but you're being late so often is quite bothersome."

"Ya, I know boss, and I am vorking on it."

"Well good, you are a team player. That's what I like to hear."
"It's odd though your coming in late. I know you're retired from the Armed Forces. What did they say if you <u>came</u> in late there?"

"They said, "Good morning, Admiral, can I get yer coffee sir?"

Divorced

Ole and Lena got divorced for religious reasons. She worshipped money and he didn't have any.

Just for the Rice

Ole said his sister was so poor she got married just for the rice.

The Pub

Ole was bragging in the pub about his eldest son and telling anybody willing to listen just how perfect he was. "He doesn't smoke, he doesn't drink alcohol and he never comes home late," said the proud Ole.
"How old is this vonderful son?" inquired Lars who was at the bar. "Oh, he vill be six months old next Tuesday," replied Ole.

Baby Shoes
Ole said that my father and mother did not love me because they bronzed my baby shoes when my feet were still in them.

Vacation
Ole dropped dead the moment he arrived home from a vacation in the Hawaiian Islands. He was laid out in the coffin for friends and neighbors to pay their respects. "He's got a really good tan," Tina from next door mused. "Da vacation did him da vorld of good. And he looks so calm and serene," said Myrtle. "That's because he died in his sleep." Explained Lena, "and he doesn't know he's dead yet, but vhen he vakes up, da shock vill kill him!"

Cold
When Lars and Ole met each other on the street one day, Lars noticed that Ole had a terrible cold.

"Have you seen a doctor about dat cold?" he asked.

"No," said Ole. "But I probably should. Do you know a good doctor?"

Lars gave him the name of his doctor and assured him that he'd be in good hands. About a week later, they met again and Lars wasn't sure if the cold was really better. "Did you see my doctor?" Lars inquired.

"Oh, yea," Ole replied. He vas a really nice guy."

"Vell, did he give you something to help yer cold?"

"Sure did!" Ole answered, somewhat enthusiastically. "He told me to drink a big glass of orange yuice after a hot bath."

"Vell, did it help?" Lar asked hesitantly.

"How vould I know?" Ole reported. "I haven't even finished drinking the hot bath yet!"

Lena's Name

Lars was invited to Ole's home for dinner one evening. He was impressed by the way Ole preceded every request to his wife, Lena, with nice terms like: Honey, My Love, Darling, Sveetheart, Pumpkin, etc. Ole and Lena had been married almost 70 years and, clearly, they were still very much in love. While Lena was in the kitchen, Lars leaned over to Ole and said, "I tink it's vonderful dat, after all dese years you still call yer vife dose loving pet names." Ole hung his head. "I have to tell you da trut," he said. "Her name slipped my mind about 10 jears ago and I'm scared to deat to ask da old hen vhat it is."

First Day of Work

A young man, hired by a supermarket, reported for his first day of work. Ole, the manager greeted him with a warm handshake and a smile, gave him a broom and said, "yer first job vill be to sveep out da store."

"But I'm a college graduate," the young man replied indignantly.

"Oh, I'm sorry. I didn't know dat," said Ole. "Here give me da broom, I'll show you how."

Sven Said to Ole

Sven: I went by your house last night and saw you kissing your wife in the window.
Ole: The jokes on you. I vasn't even home last night.

Tunnel of Love

Lena took Ole to the tunnel of love, and she told Ole to wait outside.

Advantage Over Norway

Sweden has one big, big advantage over Norway. They have much, much better neighbors.

Tired of Norway

If a person is tired of Norway, they are tired of life!

Anniversary
Knute: So, I heard dat today iss yer veddin' anniversary.
Ole: Ya, ve vas married by a judge but I'm tinkin' mebbe I shoulda asked fer a jury instead.

Football Game
By the time Ole arrived at the football game, the first quarter was almost over. "Vhy are you so late?" Lars asked. "I had to toss a coin to decide between going to shurch and coming to da game." "How long could dat haf taken you?" Lars asked. "Vell," said Ole, "I had to toss it 14 times."

Hiccups
Ole goes into a drug store and asks the pharmacist if he can give him something for the hiccups. The pharmacist promptly reaches out and slaps Ole in the face. "Vhat did you do dat for?" Ole asks. "Well, you don't have the hiccups anymore do you?" Ole says, "No, but my wife, Lena out in the car still does!"

Suspense
How do you keep a Norwegian in suspense? Give him a mirror and tell him to wait for the other person to say "hello."

Chicken
Lena thinks the chicken is done when the feathers turn black.

Beauty Salon
Ole reports that Lena spent two hours in the beauty salon last Tuesday. "And," says Ole, "dat yust for da estimate."

Cooking
The only good thing about Lena's cooking is that it broke my dog from begging at the kitchen table.

So Poor
Ole was so poor that when all the other kids had sleds, he had to coast down the hill on his cousin.

Soda Bottles
Why does Ole always have some empty soda bottles in the

fridge? In case there's anyone who ain't thirsty.

Baker's Shop
An irate Lena burst into the baker's shop and said, "I sent my son in for two pounds of cookies dis morning but when I veighed them dere vas only vun pound. I suggest you sheck your scales." The baker looked at her calmly for a moment or two then replied, "Ma'am, I suggest you weigh your son."

Make-Up
Lars: Your sister uses too much make-up.
Sven: Do you tink so?
Lars: Yes. It's so tick dat if you tell her a joke, fine minutes after she stopped laughing her face is still smiling!

Minnesota Quarters
Hang on to any of the new Minnesota Quarters you may have or acquire. They may be worth MUCH MORE than 25 cents! The US Mint announced today that it is recalling all of the Minnesota quarters that are part of its program featuring quarters from each state.

This action is being taken after numerous reports that the new quarters will not work in parking meters, toll booths, vending machines, pay phones or any other coin operated devices. The problem lies in the unique design of the Minnesota quarter, which was designed by a couple of Norwegian specialists, Sven and Ole. Apparently the duct tape holding the two dimes and the nickel together keeps jamming up the machines.

Bachelor Ole
Bachelor Ole advertised for a wife. He got 106 answers including 42 from men who wanted him to take theirs.

Norwegian Lutheran Church
The Norwegian Lutheran Church had a pastor that the congregation was getting tired of. His sermons were too long, boring, and generally lacked organization of thought. The church members tried to think of ways to get him to transfer to another church. Maybe the preacher got the hint, because one Sunday he began

his weekly announcements by saying, "I wish to announce a decision I have made after praying a number of times to Jesus. This is in regard to answering a call to another church. So after taking the matter to Jesus in a prayerful way, I wish to say that Jesus has counseled me to make a move as of June 1st. Now before my sermon for today, are there any requests for a hymn?" Almost in chorus, several members promptly spoke up to request "WHAT A FRIEND WE HAVE IN JESUS!"

Vacuum Cleaner
The vacuum cleaner sales man said, "This will cut your work in half!" Lena said, "Ufda, give me two of them.

Police Station
Lena went to the police station with her next door neighbor, Tina, to report that her husband, Ole, was missing. The policeman asked for a description. She said, "He's 35 years old, 6 foot 4, has dark eyes, dark vavy hair, an athletic build, veighs 185 pounds, is soft spoken, and is good to da shildren." Tina protested, "Yer husband is 5 foot 4, chubby, bald, has a big mout, and is mean to yer shildren." Lena replied, "<u>Ya, but who vants HIM back?</u>"

Tornado
A tornado hit Ole and Lena's farmhouse just before dawn. It lifted the roof off, picked up the beds on which Ole and Lena slept, and set them down gently in the next county. Lena began to cry. "Don't be scared, Lena," Ole said. "Ve are not hurt." Lena continued to cry. "I'm not scared," she said between sobs. "I'm happy 'cause this is da first time in 15 yrs ve've been out togedder."

Married
Ole told Sven that he was a man of few words. Sven replied, "Ya, I know. I am married too."

Ring
Ole told Sven that his wedding ring was on the wrong finger. Sven said, "I know. I married the wrong woman."

Florida

Lena went to a Florida grove to apply for a job, but the foreman thought she seemed way too qualified for the position. "Do you even have any experience picking lemons?" he asked. "Vell, I tink I do." She replied. "<u>I've been divorced tree times.</u>"

Betting on a Horse

Ole is reading his paper when Lena walks up behind him and smacks him on the back of the head with a frying pan. He asks, "Vhat vas dat for?" She says, "I found a piece of paper in your pocket vith 'Betty Sue' vritten on it."

He says, " Honey remember last week vhen I vent to the track? 'Betty Sue' vas the name of da horse I vent dere to bet on." She shrugs and walks away. Three days later he's reading his paper when she walks up behind him and smacks him with the frying pan. He asks, Vhat vas dat for?" She answers, "<u>Your horse called.</u>"

110 Years Old

One-hundred-ten-year-old Lena said, "If everyone was as healthy as I am, all the doctors would be sucking their thumbs."

Spaghetti

Did you hear about the Norwegian who couldn't eat spaghetti? He didn't have long enough dishes.

Vikings

Vikings are born leaders. You are following one!

Climb Trees

I have been on this banana diet. I have not lost any weight but you should see me climb trees.

This Diet

I was on this diet and it was the <u>worst 30 minutes of my life.</u>

On the Lighter Side

A Norwegian applied for a job at the Chicago police department. He was given test after test, but could pass none of them.

Desiring to have a Norwegian in the department, as a member of the minority, the Police captain decided to try one more test ... this one with only one question, "Who shot Lincoln?"

The Norwegian answered, "I don't know."

"Look," said the captain, "take this question home and study it. Maybe when you come back tomorrow, you'll know the answer."

That night, the Norwegian's friends asked him if he got the job.

"I think I might have," said the Norwegian. "<u>Dey got me working on a murder case already.</u>"

Exercise
I don't exercise at all. If God meant us to touch our toes, he would have put them further up on our body.

I have flabby thighs, but I'm lucky, my stomach covers them.

The advantage of exercising every day is that you die healthier.

Secret
The secret of staying young is to find an age you really like and stick with it.

Mosquitoes
What's the difference between Swedes and mosquitoes? Mosquitoes are only annoying in the summer.

Hawaii
Two men debate whether Hawaii is pronounced "HaVaii" or "Ha-Waii". They ask a passerby, who answers "HaVaii." "Thank you," says the satisfied first man. "You're velcome," said Ole.

Waiting Room
The huge backlog in the doctor's waiting room was taking its toll. Patients were glancing at their watches and getting restless. Finally Ole walked to the receptionist's station and tapped on the glass. She slid back the window back, saying, "Sir, you'll have to

wait your turn." "I just had a kvestion," he said dryly. "Is Obama still President?"

St. George and the Dragon
Ole knocks on the door of an inn known as St. George and the Dragon. The landlady answers. "Could you give a poor man something to eat?" asks Ole.

"No!" yells the woman, slamming the door in his face. A few minutes later, he knocks again. "now what do you want?" the woman asks. "Could I have a few vords vith George?"

Job
Ole was applying for a job at a company and he was asked to fill out a questionnaire. Among the things the candidates were asked was to list their high school and when they attended. Ole dutifully wrote the name of his high school, followed by the dates he attended. Monday, Tuesday, Vensday, Tursday and Friday.

The Train Ride
Ole and Lars were on their very first Minnesota train ride, heading to Minneapolis. They had brought along bananas for lunch. Just as they began to peel them, the train entered a long, dark tunnel.

"Have you eaten your banana yet?" Ole asked excitedly. "No," replied Lars.

"Vell don't touch it den," Ole exclaimed. "I yust took yun bite and vent blind!"

Ole Answers the Phone
One night, Ole and Lena were fast asleep when all of a sudden the phone rings. Ole wakens and goes to answer it. "How the heck should I know, that's a thousand miles away!" he barks into the phone and then slams down the receiver.

"Who was that?" asks Lena.
"I have no idea, Lena," answers Ole. "Somebody wanted to know if the coast is clear."

The Norwegian

The Norwegian was searching frantically for a half dollar when his friend strolled by. "Where did you lose it?" asked the friend.

"Over there by my car," answered the Norwegian.

"Well, why don't you do your looking over by your car?"

"Because," said the Norsky, "the light is much better here."

Water in the Carburetor

Lena: Der is trouble vit da car, sveetheart. It has vater in da carburetor.
Ole: Vater in da carburetor? Dat is ridiculous.
Lena: Ole, I tell you da car has vater in the carburetor.
Ole: You don't even know vat a carburetor is. I'll check it out. Ver is da car?
Lena: In da lake.

FBI

One of the best marksmen in the FBI was passing through a small town, and was astonished to notice evidence of the most amazing shooting. On trees, on walls, and on fences there were numerous bull's-eyes with a bullet hole in dead center of each one. The FBI man asked a local resident about the person responsible for this wonderful marksmanship. The resident introduced him to Ole, the shooter. 'This is the best marksmanship I have ever seen," said the FBI man. "How in the world do you do it?" "Nutting to it," said Ole. "I shoot first and draw da circles afterward."

Stamp

Oslo, Norway has introduced a new stamp with a picture of Casper Ingvaldson in honor of his achievements. In daily use it has been shown that the stamp is not sticking to envelopes. This has enraged the King of Norway who demanded a full investigation.

After a month of testing, a special commission has come out with the following findings:
The stamp is in perfect order.

Dere is nuttin vrong vith da applied adhesive.
Norwegians are yust spitting on da wrong side.

Said and Done
When all is said and done, much more is said than done. Whatever you are, be a great one. Ole, a Norwegian philosopher, said, "If things do not change, they will stay the same."

The doctor called Ole, "I have to tell you . . . your check came back." Ole replied, "Vell let me tell you sumting . . . so did my arthritis."

Bait Shop
Ole went into a bait shop and asked how much the worms cost. The answer was, "All you want for $1.00." "Great," said Ole, "I'll take $2.00 worth."

Ole and Lena
Ole came home from the doctor looking very worried. Lena said, "Vhat's the problem, Ole?" He said, "Da doctor told me to take a pill efery day for da rest of my life." She said, "So vhat? Lots of people have to take pills efery day." Ole, "<u>Ya but he only gave me four!</u>"

Norway
Lena went back to Norway for a visit. Back home Ole was keeping house by himself. One day while out walking, Ole met Lars. Lars says, "Are you lonesome dese days, Ole, now dat Lena is gone?" "Vell, a little," said Ole, "<u>But vunce a veek, I have a woman come in and nag.</u>"

Broadway
Ole said to Lena, "If you stick with me, you'll be on Broadway!"

Ole and Sven
Ole asked Sven, "Where is your brother Ingvald now?" Sven replied, "Oh, Ingvald is at Harvard." Ole said, "Harvard, Vhat is he studying?" Sven answered, "<u>He's not studying anything . . . dey are studying him.</u>"

Ole wrote a note to his mother saying that Monday vas so vindy that one of the shickens laid the same egg four times.

Lena told Tena that she didn't know what to do with Ole because he tinks he is a shicken. Tena suggested that Lena take Ole to the doctor. Lena replied, "I know . . . but we need da eggs."

Ole reported that he had a nightmare . . . his vife and Dolly Parton were fighting over him and his vife won.

Sven, Lars and Ole

Three Norwegians went down to Mexico to celebrate college graduation, got drunk, and woke up in jail, only to find that they were to be executed in the morning, though none of them can remember what they did the night before.

The first one, Sven, is strapped in the electric chair, and is asked if he has any last words. He says, "I yust graduated from Luther College and believe in the almighty power of God to intervene on the behalf of the innocent." They throw the switch and nothing happens. They all immediately fall to the floor on their knees; beg for Sven's forgiveness, and release him.

The second, Lars, is strapped in an give his last words, "I yust graduated from St. Olaf College and I believe in the power of justice to intervene on the part of the innocent." They throw the switch and, again, nothing happens. Again, they all immediately fall to their knees, beg for his forgiveness, and release him.

The last one, Ole, is strapped in and says, "Vell, I'm from the Concordia College in Moorhead, Minnesota and just graduated with a degree in Electrical Engineering, and I'll tell ya right now, ya ain't gonna electrocute nobody if you don't plug this thing in!"

Doors

When arriving at a customer's home, always use the side or back door. If the side door is in the garage and the garage door is closed then you have to go to the front door. Most of your customer's friends come to the side or back door.

When a Customer Stands You Up

If a customer stands you up, do not leave a note or call them. When someone else stands you up in that same neighborhood, stop back and see the customer. When you know you are talking to the customer you had the appointment with say, "My name is Jerry Otteson and I am here to apologize to you." The customer will ask why. Tell them, "A week ago Tuesday I thought I had an appointment with you at 6:00 p.m. but when I got here no one was home. I'm sorry." The customer will stammer for the first time in their life. Then shake your head up and down, smile and say, "You will be home for a little while now, won't you?" This is an assumption rather than a question. You will be able to give a demo to 95% of these customers because they feel guilty since they know they stood you up.

It Pays to Ask

A customer called me and ordered a classic #1769DD CUTCO hunting knife and sheath for her son for Christmas. I gave her the price and she said that it was fine. I asked her how many sons she had and she answered, "Two." I asked her if her other son hunted as well. She replied, "Yes." I asked her if she shouldn't get a CUTCO hunting knife for him also. She said, "You are right. Make it two." Then I asked if her husband hunted. She said, "Yes," then I paused dramatically. **I asked her if she had ever seen a grown man cry.** She really laughed and told me to make it three. She thanked me for helping her with her Christmas shopping. Now that is selling and product conviction. How is your product conviction? Humor sells!

The above picture was taken in 1966 of the workers in the CUTCO Cutlery factory in Olean, New York. They are singing the CUTCO Spirit song. The CUTCO factory is the place to work in the Olean area. Four years ago, I went through the CUTCO factory for the 46th time. I could give tours. <u>Whenever I come out of the CUTCO factory, I have chills up and down my spine. CUTCO is that good.</u>

How to Keep a Norwegian Busy

<u>Turn this picture over.</u>   <u>Turn this picture over.</u>

Car Meetings

Erick Laines' son, Peter, lived in Appleton, Wisconsin. Since Erick was visiting Peter and he had to be at the same CUTCO meeting in Milwaukee as I did, I asked him if he would like to ride with me. I promised Erick that we would have a great car meeting. What is a car meeting? It is a meeting you have in a car. Erick and I have been friends for years. He calls me a dumb Norwegian and I call him a flaky Finn Lander. You can't do that if you do not like and respect one another. One of the many reasons Erick is so good is because he graduated from the University of Wisconsin – Madison.

The Happy Norwegian and his CUTCO Cutlery.

I love my job. I love my job. I love my job.

Prospects vs. Suspects

A prospect is anyone that has the ability to buy. A suspect is anyone that does NOT have the ability to buy. Do not call on suspects. Sixty years ago, the best close was a good prospect. It is just as true today.

CUTCO Owner Close

Say to any customer that is a CUTCO owner:

"Many people are investing in a service of CUTCO for each of their children. Most gifts people give either go out of style or wear out within a year or two and then are forgotten forever. When you give them CUTCO, they will thank you many times a day — every time they use the CUTCO — for the rest of their lives. This is the way it always goes. Investing in a set of CUTCO for each of your children is the best thing you can do for them that money will buy. How does this sound to you?"

In CUTCO
We do not just want your business/ We want to earn it!

Only and Just
Whenever you quote a price, say "only" or "just." I have had customers say to me, "Jerry, why do you say only or just before you quote any prices?" My answer is, "Because there is no word better than only or just. If you come up with a better word, I will use it."

Erick J. Laine
Erick Laine is the majority owner of our great company, CUTCO.

CUTCO Without Jerry
A young, very intelligent CUTCO manager said, "What would CUTCO Cutlery be without Jerry Otteson?" Are you really 85? People have asked me if I am really 85. I tell them that I am not 85. I am 85 with 60 years of experience.

Good Start
When a new CUTCO sales rep has sold, for example, $7,000 in his or her first 10 days in the CUTCO business, do not say that it is wonderful. Instead, tell them that it is a good start. This should be said even if they sold $10,000 in the first 10 days.

Masterpiece
Before every demo I have ever made, every CUTCO workshop, and every CUTCO message, I say to myself, "Self, make this your masterpiece. Make it the best one you have ever done." Unfortunately, not all of them have been masterpieces but they have all been better than they would have been if I had not said this to myself.

Positive People

I am one of the most positive people you will ever meet. Who can I encourage today? Winston Churchill's best speech was only six words long. *Neva, neva, neva, give up — neva.*

CUTCO

With CUTCO, the only thing we do not cut is corners. You only have to be really great at one thing — CUTCO — and you will be successful. What a country! What a product! What a company!

Sales Tips and Ideas

1. Say to your customers, you are sharp like CUTCO. (You can't be sharper than that.) Your customers will laugh and like it.
2. Saving money looks good on you.
3. When they say they like the cheese knife, you say, "How many?" Sometimes they say two, three, four, or five. Then ask, "What else do you like?." If they say they like the peeler, you again ask, "How many?" I keep saying what else and how many until they stop me. Then I say, "Let's save something for the next time." This is assuming there will be a next time.
4. Tell anyone you call on that has CUTCO to please tell everyone how much you like your CUTCO.
5. Always say "your paring knife" or "your trimmer" because you assume it will be theirs.
6. Tell your customer that if they could see a wood-handled knife that has been used for a while under a microscope they would never use that knife again. There are more bacteria in that knife handle than in a toilet.
7. You can only use the next one if you have 100% product conviction. When your customer brings out their favorite two knives, you look the customer in the eye and say, "You really do need good cutlery, don't you?" This is not a questions but an assumption. Often at this point, the customer will agree with you and after this you will not get the objection that they do not need CUTCO.
8. Give the customer one or two sincere compliments. Make sure they are sincere compliments. The best things you can compliment a customer on are their children and pets.
9. CUTCO is not expensive — it is priceless.

10. Be proud you are a CUTCO salesperson. You should be proud of any product or service you are selling.
11. Life taken by the inch (day) is a cinch. Life taken by the mile (year) is a trial.
12. The best sermon is a good example.
13. Don't just sit there — buy something.
14. Never trust anyone whose stomach does not move when they laugh.

Your CUTCO Is So Good

Tell your customer, that their CUTCO is so good that even when it is dull it is better than most other knives even when they are sharp. World famous <u>CUTCO</u> <u>knives</u> are made in the good old United States, not some foreign country. This is more important than it was a year ago. It will be more important a year from now than it is now. <u>The CUTCO cheese knife is so sharp, it will cut cheese so thin, there is only one side to it!</u>

Field Training — A Phenomenal Success

A CUTCO manager recently said, Jerry Otteson has been selling CUTCO for over sixty years. He attributes his longevity to field training. Over sixty years later, here are some of Jerry's thoughts on field training:

When I first started, there was no such thing as three-day training seminars, there was only field training. This is how representatives learned the business; then we taught them to write orders.

They used to call me <u>Jerry 'Field Training' Otteson</u>. I would some-times take up to six people on field training. I scheduled about 40 demos a week and took someone field training on almost every demo.

I preached field training at every meeting. If anyone has a grand day, we used to say, '<u>Who saw you sell it?</u>' In the past, we believed that a grand day was only exciting if you were field training on it.

Field training is the biggest reason the company is booming today. Field training makes you try harder and makes you more enthu-siastic. You will sell twice as much when you are field training. I made more appointments because I knew that I had to show someone the business. Field training is a win-win situation for both the trainer and the trainee.

People learn more on field training where I did not sell anything. I would always tell people you might see me sell $1,000 or might not see me sell anything but you will see me work.

When we arrived at the customer's home, I explained that we are training and that the trainee will just be observing and will not be participating in the demo. Always have them take notes because it will help them to remember twice as much. Tell them to only say hello and goodbye and that is all. And have them sit back away from the table because all the attention should be on you during the demo.

I think that field training is a tremendous development tool. You will develop two times as many top people with field training. When you help people do well they stay in our business for a long time.

If you do the right things in your office people will beg to go on field training with you. If you are positive, have done at least two demos and have appointments scheduled, you can be a great field trainer. You don't need to sell a lot to be a good field trainer.

The people are what Jerry loves the most about Vector, in addition to the product and the company. He has sold over $2,000,000 CUTCO retail. And he has field trained over 3,000 people. His goal in life is to always develop people to be better than he is.

Jerry, thank you for all your hard work over the years and especially for Making a difference!

Vector Marking Corporation
CUTCO

Advice
- You have to learn how to lose before you can learn how to win.
- If all you have is a hammer, everything looks like a nail.

- Bloom where you are planted.
- Some people are young at 80 and some are old at 20.
- Are you talking success? If not, why? You can't prepare for failure and be successful.
- If you are talking and thinking success, I will see you at the top.
- Do not make plans for the worst — make plans for the best.
- The three C's to be successful in life: character, competence and chemistry.
- A leader knows what needs to be done and she/he does it.
- If you eliminate "could have," "would have" and "should have," you will have a happy life.
- It does not matter how smart you are if people do not like you.
- Life is good.
- You do not stop laughing because you grow old; you grow old because you stop laughing.
- The good news is the bad news is not true.
- In order to teach, you have to learn.
- If you are looking for a helping hand, look at the end of your arm.

Laugh
Laugh a lot and you'll live a long and happier life. Can you laugh at yourself?

Laugh on Credit
Even if there is nothing to laugh about, laugh on credit.

Did You?
Did you tell your wife at least once every day that you love her? If not, why not?

Ken Schmidt
Ken Schmidt sold over half a million dollars in CUTCO personally from January 1, 1980 to December 31, 1981. That is $1,000 a day for five days a week for two years. With today's inflation that would be over one million dollars at today's CUTCO prices. His only customers were the Houston, Texas Fire Department. Ken called in 2006 and my wife Donna answered the phone. He said,

"This is Ken Schmidt. Do you remember me?" Donna said, "No."
He said, "I am the tall, young, good-looking one." Without hesitation, Donna replied, "**Are you still tall?**" Ken is one of the best salesmen I have ever known. I am proud that I was his CUTCO division manager for four years.

Look Good or Feel Good

Someone once asked me if I would rather look good or feel good. Most of you reading this book have both. I would rather feel good than look good. We all know many people that look good but don't feel good. I have a lot of living to do and so do you.

Fargo, North Dakota and Appleton, Wisconsin

I was a CUTCO division manager for three years in Fargo and 24 years in Appleton. As a manager I never gave anyone hell. That does not mean I did not meet with managers and get done what had to be done. Giving people hell does not work. It never has and it never will. If you give someone hell the first time, things do not go well. They will feel that life is too short to work with this manager and quit.

Attitude

How is your attitude? When will you become positive automatically? That is when you are positive without thinking about it. When this becomes part of you automatically, you will have the world by the tail with a downward pull.

Twelve Points on Attitude

1. It is your attitude at the beginning of a task more than anything else that will determine your success or failure.
2. It is your attitude towards life that will determine life's attitude towards you. Despite many people's belief to the contrary, life plays no favorites.
3. You control your attitude. If you are negative it is because you have decided to be negative and not because of other people or circumstances.
4. Act as if you have a good attitude. Remember actions trigger feelings just as feelings trigger actions.
5. Before a person can achieve the kind of results he wants, he must first become that person. He must then think, walk,

talk, act and conduct himself in all of his affairs, as would the person he wished to become.

6. Treat everybody as the most important person in the world.
7. Attitudes are based on assumptions. In order to change attitudes one must first change one's assumptions.
8. Develop the attitude that there are more reasons why you should succeed than reasons why you should fail.
9. When you are faced with a problem, adopt the attitude that you can and will solve it.
10. We become what we think about. Control your thoughts and you will control your life.

Attitude

The longer I live, the more I realize the impact of attitude on life. Attitude, to me, is more important than facts. It is more important than the past, than education, than money, than circumstances, than failures, than successes, than what other people think, say or do. It is more important than appearance, giftedness or skill. It will make or break a company, a church, or a home. The remarkable thing is, we have a choice every day, regarding the attitude we will embrace for that day. We cannot change the inevitable. The only thing we can do is play on the one string we have, and that is our attitude. I am convinced that life is 10% what happens to me, and 90% how I react to it. And so it is with you . . . we are in charge of our attitudes! Keep smiling!

Develop

If you are a sales manager and you want to develop three to four times as many great managers, try this. Every Monday through Saturday morning, list the first, second, third, fourth and fifth potential managers you are working with. On Friday, the one that was fourth on Monday may be the first on Friday. Try this. You will like the results. It works because it keeps you checking the right things. It also helped me develop many great managers from my CUTCO pilot.

Develop People

I was taught to develop people that are better than I am. I have done it a few times: <u>Don Lund, Marty Domitrovich, Ken Schmidt, Denny Mahoney, and Carlton Lund.</u> Marty Domitrovich, Ken

Schmidt and I helped develop Don Muelrath. Marty Domitrovich and I developed Tom Rastrelli and Curt Holub. Ken Schmidt and I developed Tom Koehler. Ken Schmidt and I developed Rick Fenzl. Ken Schmidt, Rick Fenzl and I developed Larry Riechers. <u>Do not let your ego keep you from developing people that are better than you are.</u>

Long Day

What is a long day? It is when you start early and you work late. I have worked long days with Marty Domitrovich, Tom Rastrelli, Danny Lewis, Denny Mahoney and Jamie Zimbroff.

What do you say to a good prospect that is really cold to you over the phone or when you get to the prospect's home? You say "Have you had a bad experience with a salesperson?"
When the customer says, "<u>Have I ever!</u>" ask them to tell you about it. Let them ramble or rave for two or three minutes and then say, "You have a lot more patience than I would have. <u>Let me show you that all salespeople are not like that one.</u>" This helps clear the air. If you do not do this, you will never, ever sell to this prospect no matter how good you are. After you have cleared the air, you will sell to more than half of these people.

Very Few

I have very few original ideas. I take other people's ideas and use them. This was my idea.

When I first started with CUTCO, I had some customers tell me to leave my card and they would call me. Nobody ever called. So I made cards that were blank on one side and on the other it said, "Don't just sit there . . . buy something!" The next time a customer asked me to leave a card, I handed them one of my new cards with the blank side up. I then asked them to turn it over. Not just a few customers laughed. Not just some laughed. They all laughed and many of them invested in CUTCO. Humor and product conviction sells. How is your sense of humor? How is your product conviction?

Confidence

Each morning for the past 60 years, I have said to myself, "<u>I am</u>

healthy. I am excited. I am great." Some people tell me that they can do the first two with no problem but they have a problem with the third — I am great. That is the most important one. If you do not think you are great nobody else will. We all like people who are confident but not arrogant. Be confident!

We Can't

We can't fix it if we do not face it.

Heroes

Many young people today don't have a hero. This is a big, big mistake. I have five heroes:

1. My father, who was the best salesman I have ever known. I could not have had a better father. I learned a lot from him.
2. Marty Domitrovich, who is the greatest person I have ever known. Marty was 20 years younger than me. Where is it written that one of your heroes can't be younger than yourself?
3. B. G. Brekken, who was the best CUTCO division manager I have ever known. He recruited, trained, challenged and inspired me. He called me every morning at 9:00 a.m. (except Sunday) for eleven months until I became a CUTCO division manager. The "G" in B.G. stands for great.
4. Ray Deardorff, who was my first regional manager in Minneapolis, Minnesota. He was wonderful.
5. Erick Laine, majority owner of CUTCO. Erick saved our company. **Thanks, Erick!**

Trouble Tree

This is a story I've always found inspirational.

The carpenter I hired to help me remodel my home had just finished a rough first day on the job. A flat tire had made him lose an hour of work, his electric saw quit, and then his ancient pickup truck refused to start.

While I drove him home, he sat in stony silence. On arriving, he invited me in to meet his family. As he walked toward his house, he paused briefly at a tree near the walk, touching the tips of the branches with both hands. Then, opening the door, he underwent an amazing transformation. His tanned face wreathed in smiles, and he hugged his two small children and gave his wife a kiss.

Afterward, he walked me to the car. We passed the tree and my curiosity got the better of me. I asked him about what I had seen him do earlier. "Oh, that's my trouble tree," he replied. "I know I can't help having them on the job, but one thing's for sure — troubles don't belong in the house with my family. So I just hang them on the tree every night when I come home; then in the morning I pick them up again. Funny thing," he said, smiling. <u>"When I come out in the morning to pick them up, there aren't nearly as many as I remember hanging up the night before."</u>

Two People
If two people make a deal (for example, Joe Cardillo and myself) and it is good for me but not for Joe, he will never deal with me again. And he shouldn't. If the deal is good for Joe and not for me, I will never deal with him again. Many people in sales have never figured this out. I learned this from my father 65 years ago. Joe is a wonderful manager, and he has a great wife Jenn.

Fi and Bob Mazanke
Fi and Bob Mazanke have been great friends of mine for many years. Fi has coached many CUTCO managers and also many non-CUTCO people. She is the best coach of anyone I have ever seen. Bob is also great and very, very successful in business. They have two wonderful children: Alexandra and Jake.

Nice Matters - Kathy Hanegraaf
"Nice matters" came from my new Cutco customer and friend, Kathy Hanegraaf, from Waupaca, Wisconsin. Yes, nice does matter.

Alexandra Mazanke's Letter
This is a copy of a letter that I got for my birthday a couple years ago from Alexandra, Bob and Fi's daughter, who was twelve years old.

Dear Jerry,
What is your middle name? I hope it is not hip and trendy because
you are too old to have a hip and trendy name. Happy Birthday
Jerry.

Alexandra Mazanke

Who Saw You Sell It
If you are in sales, you will sell over 50% more when field training versus calling on the same prospects by yourself.

Made in the United States
Have you tried to buy clothes made in the United States lately? It is almost impossible. There has not been a TV set made in the United States for over 40 years. People crave getting something great made in the good old USA.

Modest
One day, someone said to me, "Jerry, you are very modest." Then they said, "You have a lot to be modest about!"

Ice Cream Is Good for the Soul
Years ago I took my children to a restaurant. My six-year-old daughter asked if she could say grace. As we bowed our heads, she said, "God is good, God is great. Thank you for the food, and I would even thank you more if dad gets us ice cream for dessert. And liberty and justice for all! Amen!"

Along with the laughter from other customers nearby, I heard a woman remark, "That's what's wrong with this country. Kids today don't even know how to pray. Asking God for ice cream! Why, I never!"

Hearing this, my daughter burst into tears and asked me, "Did I do it wrong? Is God mad at me?"

As I held her and assured her that she had done a terrific job and God was certainly not mad at her, an elderly gentleman approached the table. He winked at my daughter and said, "I happen to know that God thought that was a great prayer."

"Really?" my daughter asked. "Cross my heart," the man replied. Then in a theatrical whisper he added (indicating the woman whose remark had started this whole thing), "Too bad she never asks God for ice cream. A little ice cream is good for the soul sometimes."

Naturally, I bought my kids ice cream at the end of the meal. Our daughter stared at hers for a moment and then did something I will remember the rest of my life. She picked up her sundae and without a word, walked over and placed it in front of the woman. With a big smile she told her, "Here, this is for you. Ice cream is good for the soul sometimes, and my soul is good already."

John Kane – My CUTCO Son
John was in charge of the national F.S.M. meeting in Hollywood, California. I have never seen a better-run meeting thanks to John. I really learned a lot from him. John is in a class all by himself. Tracy Kane is great also.

Angie and Warren MacDougall
Angie is a great CUTCO division manager in Calgary, Canada. Her husband Warren is just as good as Angie. I knew Angie and Warren were great the first time we met — and I was right. When you are right, you have a big, big advantage.

Jeff and Debbie Bry
Jeff is one of the good guys. He is pure Norwegian. Jeff says the hardest thing about being Norwegian is not bragging about it. Jeff has more friends than any man I know and he deserves them.

Ernie Cooper
Ernie is one of the best friends I have ever had. We were fellow CUTCO division managers. He was in Columbus, Ohio and I was in Appleton. Ernie developed many great managers since he was a wonderful teacher. He drove hundreds of miles to see me for just half a day. Now that's a friend. Ernie called me a "lost Norwegian" and I called him a "hillbilly." Whenever we saw each other we laughed full time.

Ernie started an insurance agency in Columbus, Ohio from scratch. The third year, Ernie made $200,000 and that was 30 years ago. At today's prices, that would be over half a million dollars.

Ernie has been in heaven for the past 30 years and I still think about him almost every day.

The Famous Shirt Story

The other day, I went to a big, big department store in Appleton to buy a shirt. There were six clerks in the back of the store talking and they completely ignored me. I have a lot of patience but I finally said, "Will someone please wait on me?" This surly clerk came up to me and said, "What do you want?" I gulped and said, "I'd like an 18 — 32 white Calvin Klein designer shirt. Do you have one?" He said, "I doubt it but if you insist, I will look. We got a shipment of shirts today." I told him to forget it. I was so discouraged with his lack of courtesy and enthusiasm. Instead of buying a shirt, three suits, three sport coats, two overcoats and other clothing, I bought nothing.

I took a short cut to my car and went down this alley. The most enthusiastic person I had ever seen grabbed me by the arm and said, "Have I got a deal for you in my men's clothing store." I asked where his store was located. He said, "Right here." It was the smallest store I have ever seen. I asked him if he had shirts. He said, "Do we have shirts!" I said, "I want a white Calvin Klein designer shirt in size 18 — 32. Do you have one?" He told me he didn't but that he had a shirt that was much better than any Calvin Klein designer shirt because the collar and cuffs will never wear out. It is the greatest shirt ever made.

He told me the brand but I had never heard of it. He said, "I know but you will within two years. You will hear more about this brand than all the Calvin Klein and Ralph Lauren designer shirts put together. Remember, the collar and cuffs will never ever wear out." I asked him how much the shirt cost and he told me ONLY $150. I said, "$150! Are your crazy? I usually spend $75 for a designer shirt." He told me that I was again forgetting that the collar and cuffs would never wear out and that it was the best shirt ever made.

He was so enthusiastic, I got out my $150 and threw it on the table. I grabbed my shirt and ran to the car. I usually walk slowly but this time, I ran. I raced home so fast that luckily, I did not get killed since I went through stop signs and red lights. Once I got into my driveway, I ran into the house, leaving the car running and the door open. I yelled, "Donna, Donna. Come see my new shirt!" She said, "What is so special about this shirt?" I told her that the collar and cuffs will never wear out and it was the best shirt ever made. Donna told me that she had never heard of that brand shirt before. I said, "I know you haven't but within two years you will hear more about this brand than all the Calvin Klein and Ralph Lauren designer shirts put together. The collar and cuffs will never wear out." Then Donna asked me how much it cost. I told her only $150. She said, "Are you crazy? You usually spend $75 for a dress shirt." I said, "Donna, you are forgetting that the collar and cuffs will NEVER wear out. It is the best shirt ever made." (Donna is Scottish.)

In 1990 in Olean, New York, I told the "Famous Shirt Story." I jumped on the table, threw my sport coat in the audience as far as I could, and spun around the table showing what my new shirt looked like after one washing. The audience laughed for three minutes.

I recruited that salesman, thinking that if he could sell me that lousy shirt for $150 then think how well he will do selling World Famous CUTCO Cutlery. Those signs do not say "Exit." They say, "Excite." Let's get so excited that you sell more in the next five weeks than you did the last five months.Thirty-five years ago, I told this shirt story to over 1,500 CUTCO managers and sales reps in San Francisco. I met a CUTCO manager at this meeting and did not see him again for fifteen years. I introduced myself and asked if he remembered me. He said, "Remember you? Of course I do. You gave the shirt story on enthusiasm that I will never forget." Many people forget many talks that I gave but they will never forget the shirt story.

Jerry telling the "Famous Shirt Story" in Olean, New York Jerry's shirt after one washing.

Today
This is the beginning of a new day.
I can waste it or use it for good.
What I do today is important because
I am exchanging a day of my life for it.
When tomorrow comes, this day will be
Gone forever, leaving in its place
Something I have traded it for.
I want it to gain; I want it to be good,
I want it to be a success; I want it to be prosperity;
In order that I shall not regret the price I paid for today!

Success
To laugh often and love much;
to win the respect of intelligent persons
and the affection of children;
to earn the approbation of honest critics
and endure the betrayal of false friends;
to appreciate beauty;
to find the best in others;
to give of one's self;
to leave the world a bit better.
whether by a healthy child,

a garden patch
or a redeemed social condition;
to have played and laughed with enthusiasm
and sung with exaltation;
to know even one life has breathed easier
because you have lived – this is
to have succeeded!

That's Not My Job
This is a story about four people named Everybody, Somebody, Anybody and Nobody. There was an important job to be done and Everybody was sure that Somebody would do it. Anybody could have done it, but Nobody did it because it was Everybody's job. Everybody thought Anybody could do it, but Nobody realized that Everybody wouldn't do it. It ended up that Everybody blamed Somebody when Nobody did what Anybody could have.

Advice on Attitude
1. It is your attitude at the beginning of a task more than anything else that will determine your success or failure.
2. It is your attitude toward life that will determine life's attitude toward you. Despite many people's belief to the contrary, life plays no favorites.
3. You control your attitude. If you are negative, it is because you have decided to be negative and not because of other circumstances.
4. Act as if you have a good attitude. Remember, actions trigger feelings just as feelings trigger actions.
5. Before a person can achieve the kind of result he wants, he must first become that person. He must think, walk, act, and conduct himself in all of his affairs as would that person he wishes to become.
6. Treat everybody as the most important person in the world.
7. Attitudes are based on assumptions. In order to change attitudes, one must first change one's assumptions.
8. Develop the attitude that there are more reasons why you should succeed than reasons why you should fail.
9. When you are faced with a problem, adopt the attitude that you can and will solve it.

10. We become what we think about. Control your thoughts and you will control your life.
11. Radiate the attitude of confidence, of well-being, of a person who knows where he is going. You will then find things happening to you right away.
12. In order to develop a good attitude, take charge first thing in the morning. Do you say "Good morning, Lord" or "Good Lord, morning?"

Jim Stitt

Erick Laine is now semi-retired at Alcas. Jim Stitt is now in charge. Erick Laine is chairman emeritus. Erick, you have done a sensational job and all of us are very proud of you. Our company is in good hands with Jim Stitt. Jim is chairman of the board.

Tom and Jill Rastrelli

We have been good friends for many years. The only person I worked more long days with than Tom Rastrelli was Marty Domitrovich. Tom and Jill could be poster children for an example of a happy marriage. Tom treats Jill like a queen and she treats him like a king. That is a sure way to have a happy marriage.

Tom is in charge of fairs and shows for our company and he is doing a great job.

MEN AT WORK
Women Work all the time,
Men have to put up signs when they work.

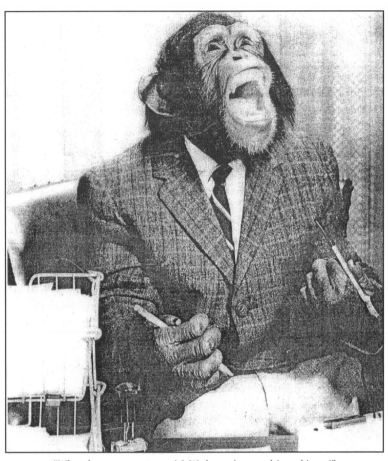

"What do you mean trace it? We haven't even shipped it yet!"

ALCAS ®
Corporation

Erick J. Laine
President
Chairman of the Board

To: Jerry Otteson

From: Erick J. Laine

Date: November 9, 1998

Re: HALL OF FAME

Dear Jerry,

You have no idea how pleased and honored I am to write this letter to again congratulate you on your induction into the Vector/CUTCO Hall of Fame. The induction that we held at SLC was such a powerful and moving experience - for all of us - that I would think everyone there would rank it as the best Hall of Fame induction we've ever seen. And as good as it was, and as great an honor as the Hall of Fame is, you, my friend, deserve them both - in spades.

Your loyalty to CUTCO and more recently to Vector could be measured in years, but it's more appropriately measured by the depth of your commitment to the product and the company, by the volume of your CUTCO career sales - and by the warmth of your relationship with all of us in the company. You truly are a great man, Jerry. You've had a great career with us and we're enormously indebted to you.

Once again, congratulations and thank you.

Sincerely,

Erick

/le

xc: Executive Board

115

VECTOR.
Marketing Corporation

Martin Domitrovich
Vice-President, Central Zone Manager

November 12, 1998

Jerry Otteson
337 E. McArthur
Appleton, WI 54911

Dear Jerry,

Congratulations on your Hall Of Fame induction. No one deserves this honor more than you. Your dedication to this business, our zone, organization and to me is very much appreciated.

Your very unselfish manner and willingness to help, even the very newest rep, is unparalleled. Jerry Otteson is the greatest inspirational leader of our time. If you need a laugh, talk to Jerry. He is the best at making you feel good.

On a personal note, I want to thank you for your 32 years of mentorship. Thank you for supporting me and my family to this day. It's been a wonderful run together and I look forward to another 30 years or so of fun. You and Donna have been excellent role models for Karen and me, plus the numerous others that you worked with over the years.

It's only fitting that a picture of your smiling face hang permanently at the Alcas Headquarters. You must be proud of the fact that you were one of the pioneers in this great business. Thanks to people like you, we have this business.

Your friend,

Marty Domitrovich
Vice-President, Central Zone Manager

January 08, 1999

Jerry Otteson
337 E. McArthur
Appleton, WI 54911

Dear Jerry,

Where do I begin! Congratulations on receiving the long overdue recognition for being a member of Cutco's Hall of Fame. Something was not right if I was in and you were not, that is for sure. I feel very lucky to have been there to see your induction and I know I speak for all Canadian managers. It was also great to finally meet you lovely wife.

You have meant a great deal to literally thousands of people in your career and I feel fortunate to have been a part of the last two directly with you. To me, you mean enthusiasm and conviction among your great many other attributes. Enthusiasm for life and for living each day. Seeing you in action and hearing about your travels shows me this. Your conviction in yourself, in the cutco program and in helping others, also is very clear to see. On top of this, you are always trying to improve which is a very strong lesson for me.

I know I am a better person for knowing you and our business is a better business because of you. Thank you. I read something the other day that spoke about attitude. You might know this, however, if you give the letters in attitude a number for their place in the alphabet, A = 1 and B = 2...., the word attitude equals 100 exactly. Attitude is Everything and yours is the best. Thanks for the guidance and thanks for the friendship.

Love,

Joe Cardillo

VECTOR™

Marketing Corporation

Don Muelrath
President
Vector West

Dear Jerry,

Your induction into Vector's Hall Of Fame made this SLC an extra special event. It was great having you and Donna with us for the entire conference. Your induction ceremony Saturday evening will provide a lasting memory for everyone in attendance.

Of all the people I know of who have been in the Cutco business, you have touched more people's lives than anyone. Speaking for myself personally, I still credit the week I spent with you when I was a young division manager as the turning point in my career (I know you have heard me say that many times - it's just as true today as the last time you heard me say it). Additionally, you are the only guy I know who can tell the same story 30 times and receive the same intensity of laughter as you received the first time the story was told. That is a very special trait.

Best wishes to you and your child bride for the next 50 years of your married life.

Enthusiastically,

Don Muelrath

ALCAS.
Corporation

Erick J. Loine
Chairman of the Board

October 17, 2005

Dear Jerry,

You are indeed a Renaissance Man! You are an outstanding sales person, superb sales manager, a man wise in the nature of other men, a humorist of the genre of Will Rogers (the Harry & Jerry CD was a riot – not all new ones but great delivery) – and on top of all that, you have a huge heart and care enormously for the people around you. I'm very, very proud to be your friend.

Warmest regards,

Erick

/le

ALCAS.
Corporation

Erick J. Laine

August 1, 2006

Mr. Jerry Otteson
337 East McArthur Street
Appleton, WI 54911

Dear Jerry,

I don't know the percentage of people who reach the age of 80. My guess is it's fairly low. What I'm <u>very</u> sure of is that the percentage of people is <u>much lower</u> for those who reach the age of 80 and are <u>still active in their business</u>, <u>still engaged in their career</u> and <u>still pursuing their chosen passion</u>. You are one of those select few.

Jerry, you've carried GENERATIONS of CUTCO and Vector people through good times and tough times on the strength of your never-ending sense of humor. To this day you give me multiple smiles and two or three belly laughs every week. You're a remarkable man, Jerry. All of us who know you admire you and love you.

Our wish on the occasion of this 80ᵗʰ birthday of yours is that you are able to continue under full sail for another 10 (maybe 20?) years. We certainly wish you the best of health and happiness for both you and Donna. You deserve it all. Thanks, Mister, and Happy Birthday.

Warmest regards,

Erick and the Olean Gang

/le

Ken Holmes
320 Thomas Street
Deseronto, Ontario K0K 1X0

Mr. Joe Cardillo
822 Barkley Rd
London, Ontario N6K 4K6

Dear Joe:

I had the pleasure once again of meeting your friend, Jerry Otteson. WOW..
I believe he could sell the steers outside the slaughter house knives and
convince them to butcher themselves.

He certainly picked me up.

Sincerely

Ken Holmes

Ken Holmes

Martin V. Domitrovich

November 2, 1947 - October 29, 2007

Mass of Resurrection
St. Patrick's Chucrh
Lake Forest, Illinois

November 2, 2007

In Loving Memory

Live Your
Dream.
I Did.
Wow!

My Life Story

Jerry Otteson is the kind of guy you love to hate. He is always in a good mood and always has something positive to say. When someone asked him how he was doing, he replied, "If I were any better, I would be twins!"

Jerry is like a magnet. He even had several waiters who would follow him around from restaurant to restaurant! The reason the waiters followed Jerry was because of his attitude. He is a natural motivator. If an employee was having a bad day, Jerry was telling them how to look on the positive side of the situation.

Seeing this style really made me curious, so one day, I went up to Jerry and said, "I don't get it! You can't be a positive person all of the time. How do you do it?" Jerry replied, "Each morning I wake up and say to myself, 'Jerry, you have two choices today. You can choose to be in a good mood or you can choose to be in a bad mood.' I choose to be in a good mood. Each time something bad happens, I can choose to be a victim or I can choose to learn from it. I choose to learn from it. Every time someone comes to me complaining, I can choose to accept their complaining, or I can point out the positive side of life. <u>I choose the positive side of life.</u>"

"Yeah, right, it's not that easy," I protested. "Yes, it is," Jerry, said. "Life is all about choices. When you cut away all the junk, every situation is a choice. You choose how to react to situations. You choose how people will affect your mood. You choose to be in a good mood or a bad mood. The bottom line: It's your choice how you live life." I reflected on what Jerry said. Soon thereafter, I left the area to start my own business. We lost touch, but I often thought about him when I had to make a choice about life instead of just reacting to it.

Several years later, I heard that three robbers had held up Jerry at gunpoint. While trying to open the safe, his hand, shaking from nervousness, slipped off the combination lock. The robbers panicked and shot him. Luckily, Jerry was found relatively quickly and was rushed to the local trauma center. After eighteen hours of surgery and weeks of intensive care, Jerry was released from the hospital with bullet fragments still in his body.

I saw Jerry about six months after the incident. When I asked him how he was, he replied, "If I were any better, I'd be twins. Wanna see my scars?" I declined to see his wounds, but I did ask him what had gone through his mind as the robbery took place. "The first thing that went through my mind was that I should have locked the back door," Jerry replied. "Then, as I lay on the floor, I remembered that I had two choices: I could choose to live or I could choose to die. I chose to live."

"Weren't you scared? Did you lose consciousness?" I asked. Jerry continued, "... The paramedics were great. They kept telling me I was going to be fine. But when they wheeled me into the ER and I saw the expressions on the faces of the doctors and nurses, I got really scared. In their eyes I read, 'He's a dead man.' I knew I needed to take action." I asked, "What did you do?"

"Well, there was a big burly nurse shouting questions at me," Jerry said. "She asked if I was allergic to anything. I replied, 'Yes.' The doctors and nurses stopped working as they waited for my answer. I took a deep breath and yelled, 'Bullets!' Over their laughter I told them, 'I am choosing to live. Operate on me as if I am alive, not dead.'"

Jerry lived, thanks to the skill of his doctors and his amazing attitude. I learned from him that every day we have the choice to live fully or not. <u>Attitude, after all, is everything.</u>

(This is not a true story, but it could be.)

In My Lifetime
In my lifetime, I have had the great honor to speak before four past Presidents of the United States. It was in 1984 on the patio at Mt. Rushmore in the Black Hills.

I Overcame a Lot
Get out your handkerchief. I had to go to first grade for two years. The first year I went to a country school where I had to walk two miles — all uphill and no shoes. This was especially hard in snowstorms that occurred even in June. The second time I went to first grade was in the big city of Starbuck, Minnesota. Nine hundred forty-two people lived in this unknown paradise. Here I only had to walk one mile to school but it was still uphill all the way and I still did not have shoes.

I have always had really bad eyes — needing glasses only for seeing. I was born with a cataract inside my eye that could not be operated on. So for eighty-five years, I have really only had one eye. Good thing I am tough!

While I was growing up, I had what they called "growing pains." My mother would rub my legs many hours a day for many years. But look how well I turned out.

I had a mastoid behind my ears. My father and Uncle Walter held me down while Dr. Giesen operated on the mastoid in our living room.

Even though I was an only child, I still was not my father and mother's favorite.

Starbuck
In Starbuck, your last name better end in "son" or be out of town by sundown. Starbuck was so small we did not have a local drunk. We had to take turns. Some did and some did not. Last summer, it was so hot in Starbuck that a dog was chasing a cat and they were both walking.

Lake Minnewaska
Lake Minnewaska is the thirteenth largest lake out of the 10,000

lakes in Minnesota. Minnesota has 20,000 swamps, 10,000 lakes, forty million mosquitoes and five fish. We lived near Lake Minnewaska.

Some of the fish we caught in Lake Minnewaska.

Pine Floats

There were a lot of Pine Floats in the Big Depression. What is a Pine Float? It is a glass of water and a toothpick.

Auction 1932

I Farmed Until I Was 6

My mother and father were farmers who paid cash rent for three years. That means they paid cash rent no matter if they had a crop or not. We were burned out (no rain) two years and hailed out one year. If it weren't for bad luck farming, we would not have had any luck at all. We sold everything we had including horses, cows, chickens and machinery and got a total of $1,600. We got $11.00 each for our best cows!

We Moved to Town

After selling everything we had, we moved to town then starved for five years. My father could not find a job for five years so he built us a house. At that time, you could buy a lot of lumber for $1,600. It was and is a nice house.

From the Tallest to the Shortest
When I was in 8th grade, I was the tallest in my class. Unfortunately, however, when I was a senior, I was the shortest. I did not grow anymore and they did. Dick Schroeder, Harry Erickson, Walt Larson and Dick Peterson were all shorter than I was. The tall ones in this picture are three to four years older than I was at the time.

Jerry and his Boy Scout Troop

Inferiority Complex
When I was in 8th grade, I had such an inferiority complex that when someone I knew came down the street I went to the opposite side of the street so I did not have to talk to them. If you know me, obviously I have overcome that problem. People like confident people. How confident are you?

I Went to Talk to My Father
I went to talk to my father, who I really loved and respected, and told him that it really bothered me that I was the shortest boy in my high school class. My father said, "Jerry, the perfect height for a man is 5 feet 9½ inches." I asked, "<u>Why is that, Dad?</u>" He said, "<u>Because that is what you are.</u>" End of conversation.

If I had a choice, I would be 6 feet 2 inches tall. In the picture above I am the one in the front row at the right end. You will notice that my friends Walter Larson, Dick Peterson, Harry Erickson and

Dick Schroeder all have full Boy Scout uniforms. I was fortunate to have a pair of pants (non-Boy Scout).

Our Neighbors Were So Poor
They were so poor that they fought the cat for scraps.

Spending
When I was in high school and college, I spent all my money on wine and women. The rest I spent on luxuries.

Ole Went to the Lumberyard
Ole went to the lumberyard. He said, "I want to buy some 4 x 2's." Sven at the lumberyard said, "You mean 2 x 4's, don't you?" Ole said, "I do not know, I have to ask my brother who is out in the truck." Ole came back 10 minutes later and said, "You are right, we want 2 x 4's." Then Sven asked Ole, "How long do you want them?" Ole said, "I don't know. I'll have to ask my brother who is out in the truck." Ole came back 10 minutes later and said, "We want them for a long time. We are building a house."

On Relief
My uncle was on relief, which is similar to welfare. My dad and mother should have been also but they were too proud. Uncle Walter had some green apples he had gotten from relief. He was going to throw them away but we told him not to, that we would eat them and we did. If you lived during or remember the Great Depression, you will never feel the same about money. Our seven daughters have teased me over the years of being tight. For example, when I get mail that has one side blank, I use it as scratch paper. They say, "How cheap can you be?" I'd say, "You can save $80.00 a year this way, and $30.00 some other way, it adds up. My dad told me the only thing you do not pay cash for is a house. I have followed his advice for most of my life. If we did not have the cash, we did not buy it.

Don't Owe Anybody!
Hugh Hamel told me not to owe anybody 30 years ago and again last week.

Are Leghorn Cows the Best Kind of Cows?
Leghorns are chickens. If people don't change their expression when you ask them this question, they never lived on a farm.

In the Big, Big Depression
In the big, big depression in Starbuck, Minnesota, we were not poor - we just did not have any money. Our neighbors were poor. They were so poor that when the wolf came to their door, he brought them sandwiches. They were so poor that when they borrowed a cup of sugar, they also had to borrow the cup. Now that is poor.

Big Bank Robbery in Starbuck
Two bank robbers held up the First National Bank in Starbuck. Our hero shot and killed one of the bank robbers with a shotgun. You do not fool with Norwegians.

Related
My Donna always said, "All Norwegians are related, if you go back far enough."

We Otteson's
We Ottesons hold our own. We started with nothing and we have kept most of it.

We Are All Sissies Now
We are all sissies now because of the wind chill. I am sure we had 100° below zero chill factor many, many times in Starbuck. When we did my father said, "If you go outside, dress warmly and do not stay out very long."

Answering Service
I have the worst telephone answering service in the world. Last month, I had just one call and they told him, "Why call him, nobody else does."

No Fault Divorces
Man to his friend – We got one of those friendly, no fault divorces. She didn't take everything. I got to keep everything that fell off the truck as she drove away.

I Was So Good They Called Me
I was so good they called me "Reverend Otteson" in Starbuck.

My Cousin Archie
My cousin Archie Otteson, who was five years older than I was, was always my hero. In those days, it cost a dime to go to the movies. Archie's four friends each had a dime, but Archie didn't have any money. His friends each gave Jack Lynch, who owned the movie theater, a dime. When Jack asked Archie for his dime, he said, "I do not need a ticket." Jack asked, "Why not?" Archie said, "I have already seen the movie." Jack explained that it didn't matter since he was still taking up a seat. Archie said, "You don't understand. I have already seen the movie." Jack laughed and told Archie to go on in. That is when Archie knew he should go into sales and he did. He did very well. After all, we are all in sales as we all deal with people.

A Social Laugher
My father Norval, Uncle Elmer, Uncle Walter, Uncle Floyd Lund and Wesley Johnson, who owned the Red Owl grocery store, told jokes by the hour. I could listen to them all day long. That is where I learned to be a social laugher.

Best Two Whist Players in the World
Most of my father's brothers and sisters were farmers and lived within a few miles from each other. Four days a week, all year long, they got together at 6:00 p.m. They ate the only thing we had — lard sandwiches without the bread. That did not take long. From 6:30 to midnight, they played the card game whist. The best two whist players I ever knew were my Aunt Agnes and my Uncle Walter. At midnight, they could tell you what was played at 7:00 and they were right. If there had been a "World Series of whist," they would have won. I would play cards twelve hours a day, seven days a week, if I could. Whist was a forerunner of bridge.

Speaking of whist, my nephew Brian Bakken and I played the "world champion" whist players at the whist store in Starbuck, Minnesota. They played as partners ten hours a day, six days a week and eight hours on Sunday. Brian and I beat them all but one game. We won one game then they won two. Then my second cousin Larry Kittleson and I played the same two and again won all but one. We won one and they won two. Brian and Larry did not make a mistake and neither did the world champions. I made a couple of mistakes, which I do on purpose so people don't think I am perfect.

Jerry wins at whist. The losers paid the winners $1.00.

Can You Take a Compliment?
One night, all of us were at Aunt Sophie and Uncle Herman Brevick's home for dinner. Aunt Sophie was a great cook. After dinner Uncle Walter said, "Sophie, that was really a good dinner." Sophie replied, "It really wasn't much." Uncle Walter said, "Then thanks for the little bit I got." Can you take a compliment? That was 70 years ago.

Do Not Try to Talk Them Out of It
When someone compliments you, do not try to talk him or her out of it. Just thank them.

How Good I Was
My father and mother told me every day how good I was and how great I was going to be in life. That is a big, big advantage over parents telling you that you are no good. My father and mother were wonderful. My father used to say, "The apple does not fall far from the tree."

Jerry's mother

The Old Man
Some of my friends called their father "the Old Man" and their mother "the Old Lady." I could never refer to my parents in that way because I loved and respected my father and mother.

The Best Way to Live to Be 100
The best way to live to be 100 is to live to be 99 and then be very, very careful. My grandma Christine Sandvig, my mother's mother, lived to be 90 when most people did not live to be 50. If you lived to be 60, you were ancient. Grandma Sandvig had twelve children and died working in her garden. She was a wonderful grandmother. My mother lived to be 97, my Aunt Betty 98 and Aunt Thelma, who lived to 102. I have two first cousins, Viola Kittleson and Elmo Sanders, that are over 100 and are still healthy. I spent many summers with Oscar and Emily Iverson and Aunt Nellie and the Sanders boys. So, of course, I will live to be over 100. It is a big, big advantage to be a "pure" Norwegian.

Best Way
The best way to look young is to hang around old people. I have done this for years. My good wife Donna reminded me that my father's side died at a younger age. I told her that I was taking

after my mother's side. My mind is made up!

My Father Got a Job
After five years, my father finally got a job. Our job (my father's and mine) paid $50.00 a month. We had two small hand lawn mowers — 12" wide. Our job was to mow the Starbuck Community Park. My father and I started mowing early Monday morning. It took us until Wednesday night to finish mowing the park. Then Thursday morning we started to mow it all over again. It took us until Saturday night to finish mowing it the second time. Sunday we set up and cleaned up after picnics. On Monday, we started the process all over again for $50.00 a month. We were glad to have a job. That is where I learned my work ethic.

Lawn Mower King
From the age of 13-15, they called me the "Lawn Mower King." I mowed 24 lawns a week. I saw green in my sleep until last week, which is 70 years later. Ed Olson, who owned the bank, was a perfectionist. If you could mow his lawn and he was satisfied, you had arrived in the lawn mowing business. Ed told me that I was the best at mowing lawns. Ed was a very nice and smart man. I got $1.00 for mowing his lawn and $1.00 for mowing Mayor Henry Nodland's lawn. Mayor Nodland later became a millionaire from the road construction business. My third $1.00 lawn was Mr. Skogland who owned the lumberyard. The others paid me 50¢ each. I made $13.50 a week mowing lawns. I also delivered papers six nights a week as well as Sunday mornings and candled eggs at the Red Owl store for three hours on Saturday nights. I worked a total of 25 hours a day, 40 days a month, 400 days a year. This is a hard record to break for anyone.

My Father Was a Master Salesman
My father was a master salesman. He sold three Starbuck cement silos in one day to three separate farmers. No one will ever break that record!

My Sports Career
When I was a sophomore in high school, I was one of the first five on the basketball team. We got a new coach when I was a junior and I was seventh man and as a senior I was the tenth man

on the basketball team. If I had played one more year, I would not have made the traveling squad.

We had a great football team when I was a senior: undefeated until we played Alberta. We wanted to see Alberta play before we played them but the coach would not let us. Alberta was ahead at the end of the first quarter 21-0. They got three touchdowns on the same play. (<u>I guess we Norwegians are slow learners, but we forget fast once we learn.</u>) We scored 22 points the second quarter so it was 22-21 at the half. We were ahead by three points with two minutes to play in the game but an Alberta man was in charge of the clock and <u>those two minutes ended up to be 11 minutes long.</u> We were robbed! As soon as Alberta scored a touchdown, the gun went off and the game was over. We lost by three points — Alberta 33, Starbuck 30. Surprise, surprise. I cried in the locker room after the game was over. I was Honorable Mention as fullback in the State of Minnesota . . . and would have been on the first team all-state if we had won that game. The fullback for Alberta was all-state fullback because they were undefeated that year.

I have many fond memories of our 1945 football team. We had a great team. The members were Dean Dahlin, Walter Larson, Gerhard "Bish" Forde, Hank Sylvester, Dick Peterson, Captain Jerome "Rev" Otteson, Dick Schroeder, Curt Pederson, Howard Olson, Dave Hagert and Lyle Hanson

Starbuck football team in 1945. Back: Dick Peterson, Dean Dahlin and Jerry. Front: Gerhard "Bish" Forde, Walter Larson and Hank Sylvester.

We Have Picked It Out

We just got a traffic light in Starbuck. When did we get it? We do not have it yet, but we have picked out the colors.

A Town With a History and a Future

In 1945, Starbuck was the home of 942 very, very happy people and one grouch!

High School

I finished in the top 40 in my high school class. There were 39 in my class. I didn't have to go to college! I went to high school for eight years.

Two Skip Days

In 1945, I was a senior in high school. Each year, the seniors were allowed to take one skip day. When it was my class's turn to take the one skip day, <u>my classmates thought if one skip day was good, two would be better.</u> So they took two skip days and took most of the juniors and sophomores with them. I tried to talk them out of it. <u>Now if you believe that, I have a bridge to sell.</u>

"Prof." Peterson expelled every one of us and our fathers had to go see him in order for us to get back in school. Smoke came out of my father's nostrils. <u>I said, "Dad, they made me do it." Thank goodness he knew that my classmates tied me up and threw me into the car to skip class. Wow, those were scary days.</u>

Prof. Peterson and Jerry

When "Prof." Peterson was 85 years old, he gave the high school graduation talk and he had the crowd in the palm of his hands in the first five minutes.

My Best Friend

My best male friend in high school was Dean Dahlin. I would go to Art and Agnes Dahlin's, Dean's father and mother's, home a lot. They were wonderful.

Dean Dahlin and Jerry – The Gold Dust Twins.

My other friends in my class were:

• Curt Pederson — Curt was one of my best friends in high school. About two-three times a month, I'd go to Curt's father Elmer and mother Mabel Pederson's farm and stay overnight. Curt had three brothers: Vernon, Earl and Dean, and two sisters: Elinor and Ilene. They are a very special family and I laugh just thinking about the times I spent with them.

• Dick Schroeder was the best-looking man I have ever known. He still is good-looking now that he is 40.

• Harry Erickson was funny in 1945 and still is.

• Dick Peterson was a great businessman.

• Gordon Hagestuen was one of the best laughers I have ever known.

Our Beautiful Lady Classmates

We all loved our beautiful young high school lady classmates. They were all very special and of course, Norwegian.

Do You Sleep Well?

My classmates asked me if I sleep well. I told them that I sleep really well at night, really well in the morning but in the afternoon, I just toss and turn.

Sleep
I sleep like a baby. I wake up every three hours and cry.

Power Naps Will Save Your Life
I have taken a power nap almost every day of my life. This is a guaranteed way to go to sleep right away every night. Unless you are sick, the following will allow you to go to sleep within one minute every night. The only reason people do not go to sleep right away is that they are thinking of something that has happened or will happen.

Just Pretend
Just pretend your mind is a basin full of water. Then you pull the plug and drain your mind. Before you know it you are asleep. Do not knock it till you try it.

40¢ an Hour And all the Cement I Could Eat
During the summers when I was 16, 17 and 18, I worked at the Starbuck Cement Products Company. I worked ten hours a day, six days a week and got 40¢ an hour and all the cement I could eat. My job was to shovel wet cement into a stave machine as fast as I could shovel it. The next summer they had two adult men do what I did alone the summer before. At the age of 16, I made $24.00 per week.

The second summer I worked 10 hours a day, six days a week. My job was to put eight bags of cement on a trolley and take it from the railroad car down into the factory and stack it up against the wall in the factory. I got 45¢ an hour and all the cement I could eat. Now I made $27.00 a week. Wow!

The third summer I got promoted and I worked 17 hours a day five days a week and ten hours on Saturday on the silo crew. I was now 18 years old. My job was to mix cement on the ground and hoist it up in a big, big pail from the ground to the top of the silo. In between I had to hoist silo staves using a rope from the ground to the top of the silo. I worked a total of 95 hours a week and made $47.50. That was a lot of money back then. At the end of 17 hours, I was so tired I had to sleep before I could eat. This is when I decided I did not want to do this kind of work all my life.

Off to College
In 1945, I went to Concordia College in Moorhead, Minnesota. I wanted to go to Luther College in Decorah, Iowa because I thought that Luther had a better football team than Concordia. My father said, "You are going to Concordia; it is closer." That was the end of the conversation.

When I got to Concordia, they did have a better football team than Luther. Going to Concordia when I did was like being in heaven. There were five women to every man. All the ladies were Norwegian, so of course, they were all beautiful. This was a given.

Mechanical Aptitude Test
I took a mechanical aptitude test in college. A perfect score was 100. I got a four. If I hadn't been lucky, I wouldn't have done so well.

Forty-Two Years
After my first semester at Concordia College, my roommate, Les Vanderpan, said to me, "I have figured out that if you keep going like you are going, it will take you 42 years to graduate." I have never been so ashamed. My father and mother worked hard to help me go to college and I was flunking out. I felt like I attended two colleges — the University of Hard Knocks and Backache University. Les' wife Norma is a great lady.

I Made Three Major Changes the Second Semester
1. I started going to class. I could not believe how much that helped.
2. I bought books for my courses.
3. I read the books.

After making these changes, I graduated with majors in economics and history and a minor in education and it only took me four years and one summer school to graduate. I only went to college for two terms: Truman's and Eisenhower's.

Four Is Perfect
At Concordia College, I was only two points from being perfect: 4 = A, 3 = B and 2 = C.

Doesn't Want to Pay for It
I met this man a few years ago that told me he was half Irish and half Scottish. The advantage of being half Irish and half Scottish is that he likes to drink but does not want to pay for it.

Jake Christianson
When I went to Concordia, I played guard (a guard is a fullback with his brains knocked out). Jake Christianson (the Silver Fox) was the football coach at Concordia and he was such a great coach. He could have been a Big Ten football coach but he loved Concordia and so did I.

Major Decision
I played football for two years and then had to make a major decision: give up football or give up girls! That was an easy decision. I gave up football.

I Loved College
I went to college right after the Big War (WWII). I would have gone to Concordia for twenty years if they had let me.

Jerry's graduation from Concordia College in Moorhead, Minnesota in 1949.

I Spent $128.00 on a 23-Day Trip
After graduating from college, three of my best friends in my college class and I traveled to seventeen different states and four providences of Canada. I spent $128.00 in 23 days. Roger Stener-

son owned North Dakota and still does. Roger lent me the money, otherwise I could not have gone. Cal Mithun, Augie Hoeger, Roger and I slept in sleeping bags in the back of the car or stayed at the Y.M.C.A. a few nights because that did not cost much. We laughed eighteen hours a day and did not have even one small argument.

During our trip, we saw the Billy Conn fight in Detroit and a major baseball game in every baseball park that existed at that time. The fifth person in the picture was Stan Hanson, who of course was Norwegian.

Back: Stan Hanson and Augie Hoeger. Front: Cal Mithun, Roger Stenerson and Jerry.

1949

While we were in New York City, we went to Coney Island. At that time it was the biggest amusement park in the world. I made the mistake of sitting in the front seat of the roller coaster. Just before we got on this rollercoaster, they told us about a sailor that had been killed a few days earlier. When you come up over the top on the roller coaster you have a tendency to rise up. This sailor rose up and was killed. I would have given everything I had or would ever have to get out of that ride. This was a wonderful trip. I paid Roger Stenerson back the $128.00 I owed him after two weeks of selling magazines.

I Taught High School for One Year

I taught high school and coached men's and women's high school basketball and men's baseball. I loved teaching and coaching except for the $225 a month salary.

141

I have now been teaching CUTCO managers and sales representatives for the past 60 years. I think good teachers are some of the most important people in America. There are poor teachers, but there are poor salespeople, doctors and lawyers, too.

Favorite Story

This is a favorite story of mine so I thought I'd pass it along. It reflects my philosophy on life — that if you help other people, you too, will be blessed.

This is a story of an elementary teacher who taught many years ago. Her name was Mrs. Thompson. As she stood in front of her fifth grade class on the very first day of school, she told the children a lie. She looked at her students and said she loved them all the same. However, that was impossible because there in the front row, slumped in his seat, was a little boy named Teddy Stoddard whom she had watched the year before. She had noticed that he didn't play well with the other children, that his clothes were messy, and that he constantly needed a bath. Teddy could be very unpleasant. As time went on, it got to the point where Mrs. Thompson would actually take delight in marking his papers with a broad red pen, making bold X's and then putting a big "F" at the top.

At the school where Mrs. Thompson taught, she was required to review each child's past records, but she put off Teddy's until last. When she finally did review his file she was in for a surprise. Teddy's first grade teacher wrote, "Teddy is a bright child with a ready laugh. He does his work neatly and has good manners. He is a joy to be around." His second grade teacher wrote, "Teddy is an excellent student, well liked by his classmates, but is troubled because his mother has a terminal illness and life at home must be a struggle." His third grade teacher wrote, "His mother's death has been hard on him. He tries to do his best, but his father doesn't show much interest and his home life will soon affect him if some steps aren't taken." His fourth grade teacher wrote, "Teddy is withdrawn and doesn't show much interest in school. He doesn't have many friends and sometimes sleeps in class."

By now Mrs. Thompson realized the problem and was ashamed

of herself. She felt even worse when her students brought her Christmas presents, all wrapped with beautiful ribbons and bright paper except for Teddy's. His was clumsily wrapped in heavy brown paper that he got from a grocery bag. Mrs. Thompson took pains to open it in the midst of her other presents. Some of the children started to laugh when she found a rhinestone bracelet with some of the stones missing and a bottle what was one-quarter filled with perfume. But she stifled the children's laughter when she exclaimed how pretty the bracelet was while putting it on and dabbing some of the perfume on her wrist.

Teddy Stoddard stayed after school that day just long enough to say, "Mrs. Thompson, today you smelled just like my mother used to." After the children left, she cried for at least an hour.

On that very day, Mrs. Thompson quit teaching reading, writing, and arithmetic and instead began to teach children. She paid particular attention to Teddy. As she worked with him his mind seemed to come alive. The more she encouraged him the faster he responded. By the end of the year, Teddy had become one of the smartest children in the class, and despite her lie, that she would love all the children the same, Teddy became teacher's pet.

A year later she found a note under her door, from Teddy, telling her that she was the best teacher he had ever had in his whole life. Six years went by before she got another note from Teddy. He wrote that he had finished high school third in his class, and that she was still the best teacher he had ever had in his whole life. Four years after that, she got another letter saying that while things had been tough at times, he'd stayed in school, had stuck with it, and would soon graduate from college with highest honors. He assured Mrs. Thompson that she was still the best and favorite teacher he had ever had in his whole life. Four more years passed and yet another note came. This time he explained that after he got his Bachelor's Degree, he decided to go further and she was still the best and favorite teacher he had ever had. But now his name was a little longer. The letter was signed "Theodore F. Stoddard, M.D."

The story doesn't end there. You see, there was still another letter that spring. Teddy said he had met this girl and they were to be married. He explained that his father had died a couple of years ago and he was wondering if Mrs. Thompson might agree to sit in the place at the wedding that was usually reserved for the mother of the groom. Of course, Mrs. Thompson did, and guess what? She wore the bracelet with the missing rhinestones, and she made sure she wore the perfume that Teddy remembered his mother wearing on their last Christmas together.

They hugged each other and Dr. Stoddard whispered in Mrs. Thompson's ear, "Thank you for making me feel important and showing me that I could make a difference." Mrs. Thompson, with tears in her eyes, whispered back, "Teddy, you have it all wrong. You were the one who taught me that I could make a difference. I didn't know how to teach until I met you."

Isn't that one of the greatest stories you've ever heard? We've all had teachers that changed our lives. Did you notice that Mrs. Thompson was a Norwegian? Of course! I had six teachers that changed by life:
Ida Erickson – 5th grade (same as Teddy)
Professor Peterson – high school
Alfield Johnson – high school
Jake Christianson – coach in college
Frieda Nielson – college
Sidney Rand – college
All six of them were Norwegians. <u>I was 32 years old before I met anyone who was not Norwegian.</u>

Sold Magazines for Three Summers
I sold magazines for three summers while in college. I knocked on every door in Moorhead, Minnesota twice. I knocked on every door in Alexandra, Minnesota twice. I even knocked on every door in Fergus Falls, Minnesota twice as well as all the small towns in between twice. Joe Neuman trained me and he was a wonderful teacher. I learned a lot from him. I lived in Moorhead and Joe dropped me off in a residential area in Fergus Falls at 1:00 in the afternoon. He told me that he would pick me up in four hours or 5:00 p.m. The first door I knocked on the woman

slammed the door in my face and swore a blue streak at me. I heard swear words I have never heard before or since.

This Was Going to Be Tougher Than I Thought
At this point, I had two choices: sit down on the curb and wait until 5:00 and quit or work four hours and then quit. I decided to work four hours and then quit but I made $15.00 that afternoon. Today, $15.00 is nothing but then it was a lot of money. A postage stamp now is 45¢ but then it was 3¢. I was really happy that I did not quit. Don't ever give up!

Don't **<u>EVER</u>** give up!

Don't Quit

When things go wrong, as they sometimes will,
When the road you're trudging seems all uphill,
When the funds are low, and the debts are high,
And you want to smile, but you have to sigh,
When care is pressing you down a bit,
Rest if you must, but don't quit.

Life is interesting with its twists and turns,
As everyone of us, sometimes learns,
Don't give up though the pace seems slow,
You may succeed with another blow.

Success is failure turned inside out,
The silver tint of the clouds of doubt,
And you never can tell how close you are,
It may be near when it seems so far;
So stick to the fight when you're hardest hit,
It's when things seem worse,
That you must not quit.

The Value of a Smile

It creates nothing, but creates much.

It enriches those who receive without impoverishing those who give.

It happens in a flash, and the memory of it sometimes lasts forever.

None are so rich they can get along without it, and none so poor but are richer for its benefits.

It creates happiness in the home, fosters goodwill in a business, and is the countersign of friends.

It is rest to the weary, daylight to the discouraged, sunshine to the sad, and nature's best antidote for trouble.

Yet it cannot be bought, begged, borrowed, or stolen, for it is something that is no earthly good to anyone until it is given away.

And if in the course of the day some of your friends should be too tired to give you a smile, why don't you give them one of yours?

For nobody needs a smile so much as those who have none left

to give!
SMILE!

The First Thing I Was Happy About
When I was transferred from Fargo, North Dakota to Appleton, Wisconsin, this was the first thing I was happy about since I didn't have to drive from Fargo to Minot, North Dakota in the wintertime. In one week, my wife Bernice and I had to drive to Appleton, decide if we wanted to live in Appleton or Green Bay, buy a house and get back to Fargo to pack our belongings and move. We did it. It is surprising how much you can get done in a week when you have to.

Act Like You Know It
After moving to Appleton, I had four district managers in our Dairyland Division (Wisconsin and Upper Michigan). Three of the four managers were in the business before I was. I had to have a meeting with our four district managers so I called Mr. Deardorff, my region manager in Minneapolis. His first name was Ray, but I respected him so much I always called him Mr. Deardorff. I told him that I had a problem. He said, "You mean an opportunity, situation or circumstance, don't you?" I said, "Yes." I felt better already and I had not even told Mr. Deardorff what was bothering me. I explained to him that I was having a meeting with the four district managers and it scared me. He told me to act like you know it and they will never know the difference. He said, "People like confident people, Jerry, so be confident."

I felt great after that talk with Mr. Deardorff and I did fine at our meeting. The four of them did not know my knees were shaking. If I had said to them that I was scared they would have wondered who this dummy was they sent from Fargo. I learned so much from Mr. Deardorff. He was a perfect role model, very likeable and a great regional manager.

Deep Sea Sailfishing in Miami
In 1954, Mr. Deardorff (left end of the picture, next page) and the four division managers (I am the second on the left) went deep-sea fishing in Miami. Four of us caught a sailfish. Les Rommel,

the one in the middle, did not catch one.

When we got back to see our wives, we told them that Les was the only one that caught a sailfish. His wife, Shirley, was so excited that she said that she wanted to hang it over their fireplace. The other four wives did not want a mounted sailfish. We worked hard and played hard. That is what I have done all my life.

Ray Deardorff, Jerry, Les Rommel, Bruce Yench and B. W. Brekken

Had to Sell the House and Car
It cost so much to mount my sailfish that I had to sell the house and car to pay for it. It was worth it since I caught the biggest one.

How Many Hours?
People ask me how many hours a day I work. I tell them that I only work ½ days: 10 in the morning until 10:00 at night.

I Got Married
I married Bernice Myhra just one year after graduating from college. Bernice majored in Music. She was in the world famous Concordia choir and played the organ and piano perfectly. She learned to play the organ first and played at the First Lutheran Church in Fargo when she was 16 years old. **Bernice was a great wife**.

Debby and me at Jackson Hole, WY in 1960. Bernice, Debby, Becky and yours truly drove to California.

I Always Wanted

I always wanted to own my own men's clothing store so I worked for Matt Siegel's Men's Clothing in Fargo. I figured out after one week that I could work there all my life and not own my own men's clothing store.

I then answered a blind ad in the Fargo North Dakota paper. The ad said to call for part-time work. I answered the ad and went to my interview. I got the job! I was really fired up and could hardly wait to get trained and start having fun selling "World Famous CUTCO Cutlery."

My father and mother owned an apartment house in Moorhead, Minnesota and I had to go through my father and mother's apartment before I got to the apartment Bernice, Debby and I rented. I saw my father before I saw my wife and he asked if I got the job. I told him I did. My father wanted to know what kind of job it was and I explained to him that it would be selling CUTCO. He said, "What is CUTCO?" Nobody had heard of CUTCO since I was the third sales representative recruited in Fargo and Moorhead. I explained to my father that I would be selling knives. I will never forget, if I live to be 120, what my dad said. As he was scowling, he said, "Nobody, nobody can make a living selling knives, nobody."

I felt like a whipped puppy. Nobody had told me that people would make fun of me for selling knives. Since I loved and respected my father, I went upstairs with my tail between my legs and told Bernice what my father had said and that I was going to quit before I even started selling CUTCO.
Bernice saved my life when she said, without hesitation, "Why don't you show him?" Eleven months later, I was promoted to CUTCO division manager and we moved from Duluth, Minnesota to Fargo, North Dakota. This is the fastest anyone has ever been promoted to division manager in the history of the company. There is not one wife in a million would have said what Bernice said.

My dad and I went to the bank to talk about us getting a loan for our first house in Fargo. The banker asked what I did for a living.

I explained that I sold CUTCO knives. The banker said, "Nobody can afford a house like this selling knives." So my father had to co-sign the mortgage papers even though I was of legal age at the time. (By the way, the house cost $16,100.) So whenever I got discouraged I looked back and remembered how my dad and even the banker said I could not do it and I did it.

It Was Hunchbacked

Our first apartment in Moorhead, Minnesota was so small, we saw a mouse and it was hunchbacked. Now that is small.

What Is Jerry Doing Now

When I first started selling CUTCO and people asked my father what I was doing, he would bow his head. He was ashamed and told them that I was selling knives. Then, my parents were invited to a CUTCO meeting where they met the wonderful people I worked with. Afterwards when people asked my father what I was doing, he put out his chest and said, "Jerry is selling 'World Famous CUTCO Knives' made in the good old United States, not some foreign country." My father's answer changed dramatically after that one meeting.

1963 Was a Character-Building Year

1. Our baby daughter Lori died at the age of six months from a brain tumor.
2. My wife Bernice died of cancer.
3. I lost half of my business to competition. I never lost anyone else to competition during my 27 years as a manager.

Donna and Basil Smith lived next to Bernice and me in Fargo. They had four girls and we had three girls. We would go to Fargo to see them, and they would come to Appleton. Donna was happily married and so was I. Donna's husband Basil was killed in an accident about nine months after Bernice died.

My mother came to live with me to help take care of our three daughters. She was a wonderful mother and grandmother and did a great job helping me. I could not have done it without my mother.

My first date with Donna was New Year's Eve 1964. I drove from Appleton to Fargo and back every weekend but two from New Year's Eve until our wedding day, April 3, 1965. I was 38 and Donna was 37 when we got married. When we decided to get married, we went to talk to Donna's father and mother to ask their approval. Since I loved Donna so much, I would have married her even if her dad and mother had disapproved. However, I knew things would be better if they approved. Ralph and Ellen Cameron were great people and very successful farmers who lived near Casselton, North Dakota. Donna's father said to me, "What is the hurry?" It was only a little over three months, but it wasn't like we didn't know each other or that we were twenty years old. Her mother said, "Nobody can take care of seven children." "Mrs. Cameron," I said, "You have seven children." She said, "That's different." I will say that it is a lot different having seven children with the same father and mother than it is to have a blended family.

Great Job
Donna did a great job of raising our seven daughters: Patti, Stacey, Toni, Lori, Becky, Heidi and Debby. Very few women in the world could have done the job Donna did. I was working over 100 hours a week at the time because when you have nine mouths to feed you'd better be working.

I Loved Them Both
Many men never had a wonderful wife and I have been fortunate to have had two of them. I loved Bernice and Donna as much as any man can love any woman. I have been very fortunate — you'll notice I didn't say lucky. When people tell me I have been lucky to have had two great wives, I remind them that I was a good prospector.

Our Lori
Our Lori said to a childhood friend from West Fargo, North Dakota 2 years after Donna and I got married, "Ever since my mother was whisked off to Wisconsin, she has not had one bad day."

2 Years Old

Stacey was 2 years old when Donna and I got married. She does not remember Bernice. Stacey said that many of her good traits, she got from Donna.

Pray for Me

Donna gave me a sign, "Pray for me. I am married to a Norwegian."

Memory

My memory's not as sharp as it used to be. Also, my memory's not as sharp as it used to be.

College and High School Reunions

I have attended as many college and high school reunions as I could. They are wonderful because I really liked all my classmates. Class reunions are where you meet the people who used to be the same age as yourself.

1970 Around the World In 37 Days /
1971 Around the World in 38 Days

I went on these two trips with Travcoa Travel Company of America. On the 1970 trip, we were on 34 different airplanes and on the 1971 trip we were on 33 different airplanes. In 1970, there were only 12 of us on this trip. Travcoa lost their shirts on this trip! Our leader was Norm from Texas. He was wonderful and we became good friends. Six of the 12 were Jewish widows between the ages of 80 and 85. I loved them. I was 51 and they called me "Sonny." "What do you think, Sonny?" One of them owned New York City, one owned Chicago and one owned Los Angeles. Pearl, the one that owned New York City, also owned a carpet business.

The day before we went into India, our guide Norm told us that he had some good news and bad news for us. We were scheduled to go into India the next morning. The bad news was that all we could have was soda crackers. The good news was that we could have all we wanted. He really scared us. Since the sanitary conditions were bad, Norm didn't want us to get Montezuma's Revenge. He told us if you buy a Coca Cola in a five star hotel have them bring it with the cap on because they could dump half the bottle out and fill it with water. After drinking the Coca Cola with water, you might die or wish you died.

We stayed on the island of Kashmir for four nights on floating palaces. One of the best carpets I have ever owned I bought in Kashmir.

We also visited the Taj Mahal. When we visited it at night, the sky was clear with a full moon. It is now closed at night because they worry about someone blowing it up. <u>I was there when the Taj Mahal was built so I guess I am old. They just don't build them like that anymore!</u>

Jerry at the Taj Mahal

Do Not Buy a Carpet
Before I left on this trip, Donna told me she did not care what I bought but that I shouldn't buy a carpet. So what did I do? I bought a carpet. Pearl helped me pick it out since I did not know anything about carpets. The only thing I know anything about is CUTCO Cutlery.

Practicing for War in New Guinea
These two tribes were practicing for war. I asked our tour director if they would hurt me. He said that they will have their spears out but you'll notice they are all laughing.

Jerry with tribe in New Gunea. They got me, Donna.

Now I Can't Speak Either One

When I was six years old, I could speak Norwegian but I couldn't speak English. Now I can't speak either one. Harold Lovdahl could speak such good Norwegian that they could understand him from one end of Norway to the other. Someone told him that his Norwegian was even better than his English and his English was perfect.

Every morning in Norway, we bought a fresh hot loaf of bread from the bakery. Then we bought Solo to drink (a very strong orange soda), butter, summer sausage and cheese. We ate this for breakfast and lunch and went to a restaurant for dinner. Some of the best food was at the train depots.

Norway (or the Holy Land) 1974, 1976, 2001 and 2003

Jerry in Norway kissing the ground in 1974.

Jerry in Sweden throwing up

In 1974, my good friend Harold Lovdahl and I went to Norway for 22 days with a car. We were in Sweden for five minutes. Sweden has one big advantage over Norway. They have much better neighbors.

Bergen, Norway Is My Favorite City in the World

I have been in Bergen four times. In 1974, we were in Bergen three days and three nights. It rained every minute we were there. Donna and I went to Bergen for two days and two nights in 1976 with Mar and June Wrolstad. It rained every minute we were there. In 2001, I went to Bergen for two days and two nights and stayed with my good friends Harold and Mary Pettersen in Lillehammer. It rained every minute I was there. I went on a tour to Norway, Iceland and Finland in 2003 with my good friends A. Kris and Annelise Jensen and others. We were in Bergen for two days and two nights. Once again it rained every minute we were there. I asked this older gentleman who was over 100, if it rained every day in Bergen. Ole replied, "I do not know, I have only lived here for 100 years."

Best Place to Live — Norway

For the fourth year in a row, a United Nations study said that Norway is the best place to live in the world. I love Norway. It is the most beautiful country in the world but I do not want to live there. Appleton, Wisconsin is a wonderful place to live. I consider it "heaven with a fence around it."

Norway's Olympic Performance Causes Some Intense Guilt

(Warning to Norwegians: Reading this column may be hazardous to your natural sense of modesty, shyness and humility.)

The Olympic Winter Games are over and the Norwegians outclass everybody on field and fjord. Not only did they top all nations in the number of medals, but their performance was nothing short of miraculous when computed on a per capita basis.

To capture the real magnitude of the Norwegian victory and give proper credit to others, here are the rankings of the real winners when computed on a population basis:

One Medal per:
Norway – 165,154
Switzerland – 758,666
Finland – 834,000
Austria – 874,111

Slovenia – 987,000
Canada – 2,103,923
Sweden – 2,867,333
Italy – 2,895,200
Germany – 3,349,458
Netherlands – 3,778,000

The United Status came in 17th with one medal per 19,889,307. China ranked on the bottom when its three medals came out to one per 389,873,000. (Any country of 1,169,619,000 that tells you their favorite sport is an official Olympic Winter Game will lie about other things too.)

If word gets back to Norway about this insightful new analysis, they'll be proud. Then they'll feel guilty for being proud because Norwegians are inherently a humble people – and for good reason. They are stoics to the core. The rugged mountains and harsh climate set the mood. They have no sandy beaches upon which to romp and play. They know they're supposed to work. They can't enjoy life without feeling guilty. So the only time they feel good is when they feel guilty.

Same Old Same Old
An Irishman, a German and a Norwegian were doing some construction work on scaffolding on the 20th floor of a building.

They were eating lunch and the Irishman said, "Corned beef and cabbage. If I get corned beef and cabbage one more time for lunch I'm going to jump off this building."

The German opened his lunch box and exclaimed, "Sauerkraut again! If I get Sauerkraut one more time I'm going to jump off, too."

The Norwegian opened his lunch and said, "Lutefisk again. If I get Lutefisk one more time, I'm jumping too."

The next day the Irishman opened his lunch box, saw corned been and cabbage and jumped to his death.

The German opened his lunch, saw sauerkraut and jumped, too.

The Norwegian opened his lunch, saw the lutefisk and jumped to his death as well.

At the funeral the Irishman's wife was weeping. She said, "If I'd known how really tired he was of corned beef and cabbage, I never would have given it to him again!"

The German's wife also wept and said, "I could have given him Bratwurst! I didn't realize he hated sauerkraut so much."

Everyone turned and stared at the Norwegian's wife.

"Hey, don't look at me," she said. "He makes his own lunch."

A Short History Lesson
George Washington was of Norwegian descent and he was well aware of it. He himself states this fact at a banquet of the Scandinavian Society of Philadelphia in 1782.

Washington's ancestry, on both his father's and mother's side can be traced to Ragnvald Øysteinson, Earl of More and Romsdal. In addition, his ancestors can be traced to Trond Haraldson, born 661, who was chieflain of Trondelag.

Between 1030 and 1035 another ancestor, Torfinn Sigurdsson, moved to Yorkshire, in Northern England. One of his sons, Bardolf Torfinnson, lived near York. The family took on the name of a small village in the area called Wassington. The family name was eventually changed from Wassington to Washington.

Vince Lombardi
I heard Vince Lombardi speak three times. He was the greatest motivational speaker I have ever heard and the greatest pro football coach ever. One day when I was paying for our Green Bay Packer season tickets, Vince came by and we talked for 20 minutes. He was extremely interesting. We had Packer season tickets

for 35 years.

1967 Ice Bowl

If everyone that ever said that they were at the Ice Bowl in Green Bay were actually there, there would have been more than 1 million at that game. The game was between the Green Bay Packers and the Dallas Cowboys for the NFL Championship. We did attend the Ice Bowl. It was colder than Fargo, North Dakota.

Electric Stockings

One of our daughters bought me electric stockings and I wore them to the Ice Bowl. Unfortunately they were defective. The next day, I went to Ponds Sporting Goods and told them that the electric stockings were defective. They said they were sorry and they would replace them. I told them that I do not need them today but I needed them yesterday.

Green Bay Packer Quarterback Club of Appleton

The Green Bay Packer Quarterback Club of Appleton meets every Monday morning after a Green Bay Packer game from 8:00-9:00 a.m. We talk smart for one hour and then we go home. I never say much! These men are ages 60 to 90 and really know their football. They are great people.

Green Bay Packer Season Tickets

Donna and I had Green Bay Packer season tickets for 35 years. We only missed eight games in Green Bay in 35 years. This is not a record, but it is way above average.

Knute Rockne

Knute was born in Voss, Norway and was a pure Norwegian. He was the best college football coach in history. He coached football for Notre Dame and won 88% of his football games. He invented the forward pass. Knute was a Lutheran teaching at a Catholic university. Knute was killed in a plane crash at the age of 43.

1983

In 1983, 14 of our great friends went to the Heidl House Resort in Green Lake, Wisconsin. WOW, what a wonderful time we had at the Grey Mansion.

Jerry and Donna with their 14 great friends

Rotary's Four-Way Test

My next-door neighbor, Buck Jensen, sponsored me into Rotary International in downtown Appleton, Wisconsin 28 years ago. This is one of the best things I ever did. Some of my best friends are Rotarians. Buck was a wonderful man and I will always be grateful to him for getting me involved in Rotary. Buck's wife Dorothy was also great.

> Rotary's Four-Way Test - of the things we think, say or do:
> 1. Is it the truth?
> 2. Is it fair to all concerned?
> 3. Will it build goodwill and better friendships?
> 4. Will it be beneficial to all concerned?

This is a good test for all of us to use in our personal and professional lives.

Smartest Thing Rotary Ever Did

Rotary International has done many wonderful things. <u>One of the best things they ever did was to start accepting women into Rotary.</u> When women became Rotarians, the organization got better.

Proudest Moment as Rotary President

What was I most proud of during my presidency of the Rotary

Club of Appleton during the 1995-1996 Rotary year? I was most proud of our June 18, 1996 program when Guy Cartwright was our main speaker. My good friend Colin Wiggett from the Republic of South Africa attended this meeting. Colin was the Rotary Group Study Exchange team leader to our District (6220), which includes half of Wisconsin and Upper Michigan. All five team members and the team leader who went to the Republic of South Africa also attended this meeting. What a meeting! They each gave a short talk about what the trip meant to them.

It Was a Wonderful Day

And then there comes along a day that will never be like any other. The day was June 18, 1996. We could say it was a day that was joyful, happy, warm, friendly, smiling, hugging, singing, and filled with sunshine, even though the rain was still coming down.

Representatives from the Republic of South Africa and Zimbabwe visited our community. Colin Wiggitt had traveled in our area with a group of medical personnel on a Rotary Group Study Exchange and he also talked.

Today was a day of celebration and everyone was in a festive mood. I was president and felt in fine form, keeping the meeting rolling without a hitch and adding my best jokes to the delight of all our visitors.

The climax of the program was a very moving presentation by Guy Cartwright, who received a very long standing ovation when he was introduced.

Crazy Drivers

Guy began his talk with a real life description of driving in Appleton with me. I told Guy to look at those crazy drivers (six of them) coming towards us. I was driving down Appleton Street when I realized that I was driving down the wrong way on a one-way street. I am handicapped — I'm Norwegian. It brought down the house and set the stage for a very heartwarming and sincere talk from this wonderful man we have all grown to respect and admire so much.

Guy stated that this joint project between our two districts must surely be the best and most successful Rotary project EVER. He said it was a very successful project . . . that everything arrives in first class condition and nothing is wasted. Hospitals must care for thousands of patients but the help from this Rotary club is giving them a great deal of help.

Guy told the group about some of the medical problems in Africa today such as AIDS and malaria, which are claiming the lives of thousands.
Guy and his wife, Ros, showed us slides that helped to bring the project to life. He also told us many interesting facts about his country and its progress. The program concluded with Guy saying he was very grateful for our commitment, motivation and concern for others less fortunate than us.

<u>A standing ovation and long applause concluded one of the most outstanding meetings we have had in a long time.</u>

Who Is Guy Cartwright?
Guy was a successful plantation owner in Africa where he raised a variety of crops on 6,000 acres. The second generation of Cartwrights is now taking over much of the responsibility, giving Guy the opportunity to continue his other activity — Rotary. Guy served as president of the club and was very active as District Governor of District 9250. Those who have met Guy have enjoyed his humor and have been inspired by his devotion to the ideals of Rotary.

Paul Harris Presentation
On January 28, 1997, Paul Groth presented me with a Paul Harris Fellowship. The following was his presentation.

Tonight it is my special privilege to present another new Paul Harris Fellow! One who has been a school teacher, was almost lucky enough to have started out life in North Dakota, admittedly majored in girls at college, and, with that auspicious background, has been an active leader for 'making a difference' in his church, his community, and in Rotary!

Our honoree is a living example of the Rotary motto, 'He profits most who serves the best.' It is said that he likes people, traveling, and football —appropriate interests for our area. His business occupation required a lot of traveling for most of his working years so he became a Rotarian later in his career — our good fortune!

His community involvement includes the following:
• A Director and then President of the Board of Directors of Villa Phoenix.
• Active in the YMCA which included a visit to a sister YMCA in the Philippines.
• A very involved member of his church for over 40 years where he has served on many committees and as President for two years.
• A member of SCORE, an organization that provides consulting services to small business owners.
• And in Rotary he was active in establishing and administering the Cutting Edge Award; an active initiator and participant in the stunts committee; a good promoter, supporter and packer for the Southern Africa Medical Project, especially after his visit to Zimbabwe and that district; an active participant in the Group Study Exchange in that he took a group to Turkey; an active supporter and promoter of the Youth Exchange program; President of the Rotary club 1994-1995; and currently serves as Assistant to District Governor Walt Pearson.

From the above you might conclude that our honoree is a pretty sharp person. You would be correct in that assumption, as that characteristic also influenced his career choice after teaching school in North Dakota. He joined Alcoa to help them find customers for their sharp projects. In that role he became a Division Manager for their Special Sales Group in Fargo, North Dakota, and was later transferred to Appleton as a Division Manager for CUTCO Cutlery.

Our honoree was widowed in 1963 with three daughters. In 1965 he married his wife, Donna, and they were blessed with four more daughters. By now you may have guessed that our honoree is Jerry Otteson. At this time I would like to ask both of them to join us up here. And while they are coming forward, I should tell you that I omitted one of Jerry's proud associations — membership in the

Sons of Norway! I think most of you are aware that he admits to being of Norwegian ancestry — a heritage of which he is so proud that he has visited his ancestral country four times! However, for Donna, you may not know the two greatest challenges in life. The first is parenting a child; and the second is surviving being married to a Norwegian!

So — President Chick, with our condolences to Donna, I present Jerry Otteson to be recognized as one of our newest Paul Harris Fellows!

The Story of a Great Rotary Project
Wonderful things can happen when Rotarians sit down for lunch. What seems to be an ordinary meal can develop into a seed that will blossom and grow, having miraculous effects on thousands of people halfway round the world.

The Southern Africa Medical Project (SAMP) was a result of a visit in 1991 by a Group Study Exchange team from Rotary District 9250 in southern Africa. This district includes Zimbabwe, Malawi, Swaziland, Mozambique and parts of Transvaal. The GSE team included two medical doctors from Zimbabwe — Dr. Elizabeth Gibson and Dr. Dawn Reeler. These doctors discussed the shortage in their country of the simplest medical supplies and equipment.

The following year, Dick and Chris Calder and Donna and I visited Zimbabwe and the Republic of South Africa and confirmed this need. Dick and Paul Groth then suggested that a districtwide project be initiated to collect reusable medical supplies for shipment to southern Africa. The program was designed to collect salvageable medical supplies from hospitals and clinics in District 6220.

In April of 1993, the first shipment was ready. Nearly 6,000 pounds of excellent supplies were sent to Harare, Zimbabwe to the Howard Salvation Army Mission Hospital. Since then, shipments have been sent to Zimbabwe, Malawi and Swaziland.

Since then, the name has been changed to the Sharing Around

(the World) Medical Project (SAMP) since supplies are shipped to other third world countries including Afghanistan, Jamaica, Nicaragua and Pakistan. There have been over 300 tons of medical supplies shipped to these countries.

Donna and me overlooking 60 hippos in Zimbabwe, Africa.

Nice, France

Dick and Chris Calder and Donna and I attended the Rotary International Convention in Nice, France. It was a wonderful Rotary meeting.

After the convention, we went to Italy for one week. At the Italian border, I cashed $800 in traveler's checks and got $1.1 million in lira. I was a millionaire until I bought one postcard. One half my lira were now gone.

Skal To Jerry

Here is a "Skal to Jerry," a song written for me by my good young friend, Rotarian Ken Johnston. All the Rotarians at our meeting sang this song to the tune of "Bicycle Built for Two":

Jerry, Jerry, Norwegian thru and thru,
Always has a story, some of them even true.
His record is full of service; you'll never see him nervous.
He does his best, to top the rest,
'Cause he's Norwegian thru and thru.

He loves one-liners, has trouble remembering two,
Sharp as a knife — of which he sells quite a few.
He's 76 and nifty, and acts like he's still 50.

He's never down, shows nary a frown,
'Cause he's Norwegian thru and thru.
Sure we kid him — he's got it coming, 'tis true,
He kids Germans, so they get back at him too.
He'd like to be somewhat slimmer,
His hopes were never dimmer.
He's still our friend, right to the end,
A Norwegian Rotarian true!

1991 Wisconsin Monopoly Champ

The Appleton Post Crescent reported:

Jerry Otteson, 65, an Appleton salesman, proved to be an astute real estate mogul as he bankrupted his challengers in the state Monopoly competition.

Otteson collected the highest real estate assets of all players in local tournaments held in Wisconsin over the last four years.

"I've been playing the game since 1941," says Otteson. "I'm thrilled to represent the state and have a chance at the title of U. S. National Monopoly Game Competition."

Otteson will compete in the Central Regional Championship in Denver September 22-23. The winners of the four regional tournaments and the defending champion, Gary Peters, will compete in the national championship October 20-21 in New York. The national winner advances to world competition in October 1992.

Chairman of the board

Jerry the Monopoly Champ – Chairman of the Board.

167

Advance to Go:
Otteson's Ready

(By: Pat Stenson)
(Printed in The Post Crescent – Saturday, September 7, 1991)

Local champ seeks national Monopoly title. Monopoly mogul Jerry Otteson has seven daughters — and none of them will play him. "They say I'm too tough, and they think I'm aggressive. I guess I am," said the man who qualified for the national regional Monopoly championship. He competes September 22-23 in Denver against 14 other state winners.

These days, right next to his Monopoly board are books on winning at the game — and Norman Vincent Peale's "The Power of Positive Thinking." "I've almost memorized that book," he said. "The national champions' ages have been anywhere from 10-55. But the record will be 65 now, because I'm 65!" Actually, he said, he's going to have fun whether he wins or loses. "But I know I'll have more of a chance if I think positive. I want to win and I plan on winning."

His age brought him a spot in USA Today this week on the front page in a brief article on the upcoming tournament. It turns out he's the oldest competitor this year. "I guess age has its privileges!" he said, laughing.

"A lot of people think winning Monopoly is all skill and some say it is all luck. Neither is true. It's about half and half. You can beat the best player in the world on a given day. I've had a game that any four-year-old could have won — I kept going to jail."

Encouraged by friends Bob Brunken, former YMCA director, and John Rankin, then-president of First Wisconsin Bank in Appleton and Menasha, Otteson entered the state competition in August 1989 at Rankin's bank. It turns out that Otteson collected the highest real estate assets of all players in tournaments held in Wisconsin during the last four years and that qualified him for central regional competition.

"My wife, Donna, says I beat little children and old ladies. I say I

beat people with master's and doctor's degrees in Monopoly," Otteson said with a grin. His friend Rankin tells him Monopoly is discussed — and played — at Harvard School of Business. "I think Monopoly is a lot like real life. It's helped me in business, too." It hones skills he has used successfully in sales, he said.

Otteson was manager of Wisconsin and Upper Michigan for CUTCO Cutlery for 24 years and North Dakota for three years; now he sells in semiretirement. He was a teacher and coach prior to that. "I loved it, but I didn't love the $225 a month." So he built a sales business.

Official Monopoly competitions consist of three 90-minute games. A judge and a banker keep tabs on play. Points are then totaled to determine the ultimate winner. The tournaments are sponsored by Parker Brothers, maker of the game. There are four national regional tournaments. Winners will compete in the once every four years national competition October 20-21 in New York City. The United States champion ultimately competes in international competition with representatives of more than 30 counties for the 1992 championship next October in Berlin.

Otteson began playing Monopoly back in 1941 in his hometown of Starbuck, Minnesota, when a high school friend taught him the game. He loved it. The world record game time is 101 hours. His personal record is seven hours. "I'll play any time I can find someone to play me," Otteson said. "Really, you should have four players playing — the ideal is four. I'm trying to practice a lot. I've got friends lined up to do four or five good games before I go," he said.

"I'm very aggressive in playing Monopoly — as I am in cards, too. Monopoly is my favorite game, then 500. But more people will play me in cards."
His game philosophy: "I always buy as many houses as I can as soon as possible. There are only 32 houses and 12 hotels. All serious Monopoly players will not put hotels on their property — they will go for four houses." "It is important to get a natural Monopoly early in the game, then you don't trade. If you do that early in a 90-minute game, you almost always win." Mentally, he's really ready right now, he said. "I'm excited about it. My Appleton Down-

town Rotary Club is 100% behind me. 'You gotta win, Jerry,' they tell me," he said. "I intend to!"

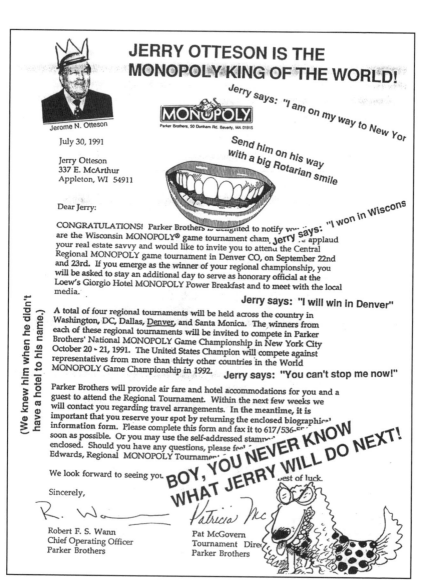

JERRY OTTESON IS THE MONOPOLY KING OF THE WORLD!

Jerry says: "I am on my way to New Yor

Jerome N. Otteson

MONOPOLY
Parker Brothers, 50 Dunham Rd. Beverly, MA 01915

July 30, 1991

Jerry Otteson
337 E. McArthur
Appleton, WI 54911

Send him on his way
with a big Rotarian smile

Dear Jerry:

Jerry says: "I won in Wiscons

CONGRATULATIONS! Parker Brothers is delighted to notify yo... ...gnted that you are the Wisconsin MONOPOLY® game tournament cham... Jerry says applaud your real estate savvy and would like to invite you to attend the Central Regional MONOPOLY game tournament in Denver CO, on September 22nd and 23rd. If you emerge as the winner of your regional championship, you will be asked to stay an additional day to serve as honorary official at the Loew's Giorgio Hotel MONOPOLY Power Breakfast and to meet with the local media.

Jerry says: "I will win in Denver"

A total of four regional tournaments will be held across the country in Washington, DC, Dallas, Denver, and Santa Monica. The winners from each of these regional tournaments will be invited to compete in Parker Brothers' National MONOPOLY Game Championship in New York City October 20 - 21, 1991. The United States Champion will compete against representatives from more than thirty other countries in the World MONOPOLY Game Championship in 1992. **Jerry says: "You can't stop me now!"**

Parker Brothers will provide air fare and hotel accommodations for you and a guest to attend the Regional Tournament. Within the next few weeks we will contact you regarding travel arrangements. In the meantime, it is important that you reserve your spot by returning the enclosed biographica¹ information form. Please complete this form and fax it to 617/536-⁵⁵ soon as possible. Or you may use the self-addressed stamp⁻ enclosed. Should you have any questions, please fee¹ ⁻ Edwards, Regional MONOPOLY Tournamer⁻

We look forward to seeing you⸱

Sincerely,

R. Wo

Robert F. S. Wann
Chief Operating Officer
Parker Brothers

Patricia Mc

Pat McGovern
Tournament Dire⸱
Parker Brothers

(We knew him when he didn't have a hotel to his name.)

BOY, YOU NEVER KNOW WHAT JERRY WILL DO NEXT!

⸱est of luck.

170

Dr. Peter Saved My Life

Two weeks before I was supposed to fly to the Philippines with Fred Hauser, I could not even stand up. My good wife Donna told me to call Dr. Peter Schubbe at Schubbe Resch Chiropractic. I called him and made an appointment for that very day. When I got to the office, I told him I would do anything you suggest so that I can go to the Philippines and he did. The trip from Appleton to Manila is a long plane trip even if your back is perfect.

When we arrived in Manila, a small car picked us up and took us up in the mountains. It was a six-hour trip on a road that would have been condemned in the United States. We were very cramped and that is the understatement of the year. The only other understatement that was as bad was when Noah said that it looked like rain.

Benny Took Us to the Airport at 4:00 a.m.

Dr. Benny Santos and his driver took us to the airport in Manila, Philippines. The traffic was bumper to bumper at 4:00 in the morning. It was so bad that if you wanted to get to the other side of the street, you had to be born there.

When we got to the airport in Manila, there were (by far) the longest lines I have ever seen. This was a Monday morning. We tried to reconfirm our reservations on Saturday and on Sunday but all the offices were closed. So we did not have our flight reconfirmed. Tak was waiting for us at the Osaka, Japan airport and if we missed our flight, there was no way of letting Tak know.

We got in this long line and I made a big mistake. I saw a shorter line but when we got there it turned out to be much longer than the line we were in. Rollie saved us again. He went to the first class counter and asked the man to help us and he did. If he had not gone to the first class counter we would still be there.

Rollie got upset with me and said, "I am sick and tired of your being positive and always saying 'no problem'." Thanks to Rollie, we got on the plane with 38 seconds to spare. We flew from Manila to Osaka and Tak met us at the airport.

171

The Tak Story

Our friend Tak from Hiroshima, Japan stayed with us two times. He always asked us to come and visit him in Japan. Tak was a Rotary Group Study Exchange team leader who came to the United States with five other Japanese young businessmen.

When Rollie Tonnell, Bret Younger and I were going to the Philippines, I wrote to Tak to tell him that we were going to be in his neighborhood and would like to stay with him. It was a long, long way from Manila, Philippines to Osaka, Japan. Tak wrote back and said that he was looking forward to seeing all of us.

The Train

We took the bullet train from Osaka to Hiroshima. The cost was $100. The bullet train went 130 miles an hour and was the smoothest ride I have ever had. Since you had only 30 seconds to get on the train, people called "pushers" pushed people on the train.

Lucky

LOST DOG

3 LEGS, BLIND IN ONE EYE,
MISSING RIGHT EAR,
TAIL BROKEN,
RECENTLY CASTRATED...
ANSWERS TO THE NAME
OF "LUCKY"

We arrived at Tak's home that cost over $2 million in U.S. currency. My room had big picture windows overlooking Hiroshima, a king-size bed, deluxe carpeting and chairs. It was his daughter's room and she was attending college.

Tak took Rollie and Bret to their room, which had no windows, chairs or a bed. They slept on the floor like many people in Japan do. Rollie started calling me "Lucky." I told Rollie that I write to

Tak once a month and he only writes to him once a year. Who should get the best room? The zipper on my suitcase broke and I asked Tak if he could have it fixed. The next day Tak gave me a new suitcase that was twice as good as the one I had. Again Rollie called me "Lucky."

Best Steak I Ever Had
Tak, Rollie, Bret, Tak's driver and I went to a small bar and steakhouse. It had the best tenderloin (by far) I have ever had. It tasted like Kobe beef. The place had only seven stools and we had taken up five of them. Rollie embarrassed me by telling the waitresses, "Keep the steaks coming until I stop you." To keep the record straight, it was not Rollie that said that, it was me.

Dollar Store
We went to the dollar store, which at the time was unique. We could not believe that everything in the store was $1.00. I asked Tak, "How much is this?" His answer was $1.00. Then I asked him how much another item was. He said, "$1.00." After asking Tak a third time how much something was, he got upset and said, "Jerry, everything is $1.00."

Three Beautiful Embroidered Framed Pictures
When I came down for breakfast the morning we were going home, Tak had three beautiful embroidered framed pictures and each of us could select one as a gift from him and his wife. Since I was the first one downstairs, I got first choice. Rollie got second choice and Bret third. Ninety-nine percent of life is timing.

Own Seven Businesses
Tak and his father own seven businesses. When Tak was in Appleton I asked him what his father did. Tak said, "He is in work prison." I asked Tak what that meant and he said that his father was a prisoner of work — he works all the time.

I asked Tak what he did. He said that he goes to their businesses and looks around. Then he goes golfing. Tak is a great golfer and goes often. The last time I golfed, I got a hole in ten. Is that good?

On a scale of 1-10, all the meals we had at Tak's home were a 20.

Tak and his wife were wonderful hosts. "Manga tousend Tak," which is Norwegian for "many thousand thanks."

The Fred Hauser Story

Fred is in charge of the three YMCAs in the Appleton area and he does a wonderful job. Fred and I were on the World Service Committee at the YMCA when they asked us to go to the Philippines in 1993. Our job was to check on the YMCA that Appleton sponsored in San Fernando. We traveled six hours by car from Manila. We did a lot of good and met some great new friends. I should call Fred lucky since his great wife Wendy is a pure Norwegian.

Fred Hauser and Jerry

The Power of a Letter

Upon our return, Fred wrote me this letter:

"I want to thank you for taking the time to visit the Philippines with me in November. We had a great time, learned a lot and became good friends.

You personally did more good in developing good relations with the La Union YMCA than you'll ever know. The United States government could learn how to be a good ambassador from you. You speak the international language of love. By using your humor you break down natural language and cultural barriers that exist between people and countries.

I appreciate your adventurous attitude and neverending energy. It was a trip I will never forget. Now it will be our challenge to deliver the story and message to our laymen and volunteers. You and I know personally the country and people we can assist."

My Trip to Russia

In 2002, I went to Russia on Carl and Leona Stapel's "Russian Waterways" trip. It was wonderful and I learned to love opera. We were on a ship for 14 nights and I sat at the same table as Chris and Cheryl Quello, Bill and Dawn Smith, and Ruth Vorpahl for two meals a day for 14 days. I enjoyed the entire trip, especially Moscow.

The Tale of Two Cows

Socialism: You have two cows. You keep one and give one to your neighbor.

Communism: You have two cows. The government takes both cows and provides you with milk. (Communism is also when you pretend to work and the government pretends to pay you.)

Fascism: You have two cows. The government takes both cows and sells you milk.

Nazism: You have two cows. The government takes both cows and shoots you.

Bureaucracy: You have two cows. The government takes both cows, shoots one, pays you for the milk and pours the milk down the drain.

Capitalism: You have two cows. You sell one and buy a bull.

The Jerry Otteson Boomerang Story

On my trip to Australia in 2006, Chuck Mandsager took boomerang lessons. My friend Chuck threw a boomerang. It slipped and hit me in the head going 100 miles an hour. They said that if I had been German, Danish, Swedish, Irish, Scottish or Polish I would have been dead. I am sure they were right.

175

Chuck Mandsager and Jerry

Oscar and Pat Boldt
Oscar and Pat have been good friends of Donna's and mine as well as many other people in Appleton. They have done more in our community than anyone else I know. <u>My life has been much richer because of Oscar and Pat.</u>

Frank Bresler
Frank and Mary Ann have been friends of ours for many years. When our television does not work, Frank fixes it. When we need a new television, Frank goes with me and helps me pick one out. Terry Timmers is also a good friend of Frank's and mine.

Jerry and Margie Ellefson
Jerry and Margie have been good friends of ours for over 50 years. They moved from Appleton to Colfax, Wisconsin and then to Hudson, Wisconsin. We really miss them.

Dick Lundgren
Dick was a very special friend of mine. Even though he has been gone for many years, I still think of him often. He was pure Swedish while I am pure Norwegian. He told me over 3,000 jokes — all Norwegian. He could tell jokes with a dialect better than anyone I knew. I would tell him Swedish jokes in return, 3,000 of them.

Marilyn Greek
Marilyn Greek does a sensational job at CUTCO'S home office in Olean, New York. All of us in the CUTCO field really appreciate her. She is the best.

Tom Wendt
Tom is the Chairman of Y.M.C.A. World Service Committee and does a wonderful job. I have been on this committee for 105 years. Sarah Miles also does a great job.

Teach People
Teach people to be happy so they don't get hardening of the attitudes.

Joseph's Shoes - Best Shoes
Perry and Jill Vanderloop own Joseph's Shoes located on College Avenue in Appleton. I buy all my shoes from Perry. I do not even look anywhere else because he gives great service. That is loyalty!

How to Stay Happily Married
Donna and I have been married for 42 years. How have we stayed happily married all this time? When I wake up, even before I am really awake, I say, "<u>Good morning, darling. I am sorry.</u>" <u>Try it.</u>

If people ask Donna how we stay happily married, <u>she says that he travels a lot.</u>

What Donna Says About Me
He really likes to travel. My wife Donna says, "Jerry does not know where he is going or where he has been but he has a wonderful time when he is there."

Jerry and Donna

Living With a Norwegian
Donna says, "Living with a Norwegian builds character." I have always wondered what that meant. I admit to being high maintenance but the fringe benefits are sensational according to Donna.

Donna Is Right
Donna always says that I expect great service and she is right. She is usually right. We would drive miles out of our way to buy from someone we like and gives great service.

We Made This Agreement
When Donna and I got married 46 years ago, I agreed not to try to change her and she would not try to change me. I kept my side of the bargain.

How High?
When Donna said, "Jump" I ask her, "How high and when can I come down?"

If
If you are married you'll agree, if your wife is not happy then nobody is happy. These are words of wisdom.

Do You Have Ulcers, Jerry?
When people ask me if I have ulcers, I tell them, "No, I am a carrier." I give them to other people.

Larry and Audrey Schiedermayer
Larry and Audrey Schiedermayer have been good friends of Donna's and mine for a long time.

Elmer VanDyke
Elmer is by far the best custodian we have ever had at Trinity Lutheran Church on Allen Street in Appleton. Elmer is also a true friend and makes me laugh.

A. Kris and Annelise Jensen - Really True Friends
Kris and Annelise were born near Copenhagen, Denmark. All of us could learn how to be great hosts and hostesses from them.

We attend the same church and Kris and I are members of the Rotary Club of Appleton. Kris is the smartest person I have ever known. When you have Kris and Annelise for friends, you can't have better friends anywhere. They invited me to their home for dinner on Christmas Eve. Have you noticed that most great men usually have wonderful wives? Amen. Kris has a great wife.

Nine Young Friends
The following nine young friends pick me up at the Heritage and drive me wherever I need to go: Kris Jensen, Hugh Begy, Frank Bresler, Bill Anciaux, Pat Lewis, Terry Timmers, Chuck Lewis, Al Olson and Sam Tralongo.

Men's Bridge
Al Olson, Bob Brandt, Les Gunter and I play bridge every Tuesday night. On Wednesdays, I play bridge with 15 ladies. Donna Olson and Ellen Gunter are in charge. They are both great.

So Old
I am so old that when I was born, the Dead Sea in Israel was not even sick.

Good for ONE HUG

FREE HUG COUPON

Redeem from any participating human being!

Hugging:
The Perfect Cure For What Ails You
No movable parts ● No batteries to wear out
No periodic checkups ● Inflation-proof
Low energy consumption ● High energy yield
No monthly payments ● Theft-proof
No insurance requirements ● Non-taxable
Non-polluting
And, of course, fully returnable

There Are Not Enough Hugs

There are not enough hugs in the world today. Redeem this coupon from any human being. Hugs are the perfect cure for what ails you. I get to hug all the beautiful young women by using this coupon. And some people think I am dumb!

Hugs ...

It's wondrous what a hug can do
A hug can cheer you when you're blue.
A hug can say, "I love you so,"
Or, "Gee, I hate to see you go."

A hug is, "Welcome back again,"
And "Great to see you! Where've you been?"
A hug can soothe a small child's pain
And bring a rainbow after rain.

The hug! There's just no doubt about it –
We scarcely could survive without it!
A hug delights and warms and charms.
It must be why God gave us arms.

Hugs are great for fathers and mothers,
Sweet for sisters, swell for brothers.
And chances are your favorite aunts
Love them more than potted plants.

Kittens crave them. Puppies love them.
Heads of state are not above them.
A hug can break the language barrier
And make your travels so much merrier.

No need to fret about your store of 'em;
The more you give, there's more of 'em.
So stretch those arms without delay
And GIVE SOMEONE A HUG TODAY!!!

M & Ms

When I went to China I took fifty pounds of M&Ms because I didn't think I would like the food. It turned out that I liked the food. Twenty-five pounds of M & M's would have been enough.

The Great Wall of China
The Great Wall of China is 4,200 miles long. I wanted to walk the entire 4,200 miles but Verlyn Ferg and Dick Calder did not. So we walked the entire wall except for 4,199 miles of it.

Rollie and Judy Tonnell
Donna and I met Rollie and Judy through Rotary. If I had not become a Rotarian, we probably would have never met and we would have missed a lot. Rollie passed away and we all miss him.

Ken and Barb Kleczka
Ken and Barb have been loyal customers and great friends of mine for years. When they come to see me, we visit for a long time. They were at Donna's funeral and I was very grateful for that!

Best Three 500 Players
Jerry Ellefson, Al Miller and John Petersen are the best 500 card players I have ever known. All three bid too high, but most of the time they make it.

Paula Basler
Paula helps me clean my apartment three hours every other week. She can do anything. She is smart and very likeable. We really appreciate Paula. She is also a very good cook. Paula is very special. I like Paula and I trust her.

Dennis Vorpahl
Dennis and I have been good friends for many years. He is the best interior decorator I have ever known as well as very likeable. He helped me move to The Heritage. Dennis died a few months ago. I miss him every day.

Ron Miller
Ron Miller is the best physical therapist in the world. He works at Neuro Spine on Michaels Drive in Appleton. For over a year, I went to Ron one week and to Dr. Peter Schubbe the next week.

Ron gave me a simple exercise to do four times a day. I did them twice a day. As soon as I did the exercises four times a day, my back was much, much better. You saved my life, Ron and I will be grateful to you for the next 20 years.

Vic Tretoskey

Vic and his good wife Julie have invested in a lot of CUTCO over the last 15 years. Vic is one of the four smartest people I have ever known and I have known a lot of very smart people. Vic and I visit for a long time every time we see each other. I liked Vic and Julie the first time we met. They say the first 17 seconds we meet someone we decide if we like them. We are usually right.

Dick and Chris Calder

In 1992, Dick, Chris, Donna and I went to Zimbabwe, Africa and the Republic of South Africa to visit Guy and Ros Cartwright and Colin Wiggett. This was one of the best trips I have ever been on. We laughed a lot and cried a lot at the poverty we saw. We also saw the greatest "negotiator" in action — Dick Calder.

Buying Luggage

In 2005, before I went to Africa, I went to Marshall Fields department store to buy new luggage for my trip. They showed me six different brands of luggage. Five of them were made in foreign countries and one was made in the United States. Which one did I buy? You are right; you are sharp like CUTCO. I bought the one made in the United States. It cost more but it was made better.

My Return Trip to the Republic of South Africa

I flew to the Republic of South Africa again in 2005. Guy and Ros Cartwright are now living in the Republic of South Africa after being forced off their 6,000-acre property. I stayed with Guy and Ros and we drove to Kruger Park, which is one of the largest game parks in the world. We stayed in Kruger Park for three nights. We saw all the animals we were supposed to see and were within a few feet of elephants.

I then flew to Port Alfred, South Africa and stayed with Colin and Louise Wiggett for 10 days. They really showed me the area. Wow, what a trip. We met Colin and Louise's best friends François and

Wendy Vosloo and now they are my friends too. We had dinner at their ranch. They are wonderful cooks. Wendy made homemade bread with a very hard but good crust. I gave them a #1724DD CUTCO bread slicer and it cut that bread like soft butter. François and Wendy raise Nguni cattle of the Zulu people. This is a breed from the past. François gave me the best gift I have ever received from anyone. He gave me a three-day-old Zulu calfskin. I have it on my office wall so I see it many times a day. The calf's mother had died from a snake bite. This calf was very important to François but he wanted to give it to me. That is a true friend.

Jerry and his new pet spot

Francois and Jerry with magic gold card

14,000 Elephants

In 2005, there were over 14,000 elephants in Kruger Park. They have to get it down to 9,000 elephants by culling them since they are destroying the park.

My Favorite Polish Person

Doug Dugal is a good friend of mine that I met through the Rotary Club of Appleton. He was born in India. When I call Doug my favorite Polish man, people laugh. Doug says he had a choice of being either Polish or Norwegian and he picked Polish. They laugh. When I tell people he did the right thing they also laugh. Anything for a cheap laugh. <u>Doug does not look Polish at all.</u> <u>That is what makes this so funny.</u>

Dennis Episcopo - A Special New Friend

I have a very special new young friend, Dennis Episcopo. He is a minister at Appleton Alliance Church and his sermons are wonderful. On a scale of one to ten, they are a twenty. I met Dennis through our Rotary Club. Dennis says it is a sin to bore people and he is right. He has a great wife — Judy.

Bill Anciaux

Bill is a true friend of mine from Rotary. Bill is interesting. His wife Marian is also a wonderful person.

Jennifer Wanke

Jennifer is a good friend of mine from Rotary. Jennifer runs LEAVEN and does an outstanding job.

Mark and Deb Gonyo

Mark is my friend from Green Bay. Mark's wife Deb is just as good as Mark. They have a daughter Emily who is very talented and likeable and will do well in life. They have driven to Appleton many times and have taken me to dinner.

Our Bridge Group

The members of our bridge group are: Jim and Mary Milslagle, Sandy Oliver, Trish Pratt and John Deising. Glenn and Dixie Guthrie helped get Donna and me into this club years ago. We get together every six to eight weeks. I am great at bridge except for my playing, bidding and scoring. We used to play bridge but now we go out to lunch and tell jokes and talk smart. I just listen and laugh. They are wonderful people.

Even If
Even if you have 1,000 friends, you do not have one to spare.

Friends
I have mentioned some of my good friends but I can't list all our friends because if we did you would not be able to carry this book.

Money
I have enough money to last the rest of my life if I don't live past Thanksgiving this year.

Australia, New Zealand and Fiji
In February 2006, I went to Australia, New Zealand and Fiji with Carl and Leona Stapel. They could not be better tour guides.

Can't Tie My Own Shoes
Rollie Tonnell told everyone who would listen, and some that wouldn't, that I can't tie my own shoelaces. This picture proves that I can.

Jerry tying shoes?

Uff-Da
Uff-da is a Norwegian saying that means that something is disgusting, awful or foolish.

Talk to Me
The worst putdown I have ever heard is "Talk to me, my mind needs a rest."

Yearly Eye Checkup

I just had my yearly eye check up with Dr. Brad Jorgenson. He told me that my eyes were getting better. I said, "Doctor, I am 85, does that mean when I am 100 my eyes will be perfect?" He laughed.

Ole and the Eye Doctor

One day Ole went to the eye doctor. The doctor asked Ole to read the chart. Ole said, "What chart?" The doctor said, "The chart on the wall." Ole said, "<u>What wall?</u>"

Heartburn

"Doctor," said Lena, "I seem to get heartburn venever I eat birthday cake." The doctor replied, "Have you tried removing the candles first?"

Ocean

Lena, said to Ole, "You remind me of the ocean." Ole said, "Ya, you mean wild, restless, romantic? Lena replied, "No you make me sick."

Wisdom of Ole

Money isn't everything. Henry Ford had all that money, millions of dollars, and he never had a Cadillac.

Yesterday

Ole said to Sven, "I passed your house yesterday." Sven replied, "Thanks."

Same Old Thing

Sven asked Ole what he was going to have for dinner. Ole answered, "<u>Same old thing – cold shoulder and hot tongue</u>."

Who Makxs a Group a Succxss

Xvxn though my typxwritxr is an old modxl, it still works quitx wxll xxcxpt for onx kxy. I havx wishxd many timxs that it workxd pxrfxctly. It is trux that thxrx arx 41 othxr kxys that do function wxll xnough, but just onx not working makxs all thx diffxrxncx. Somxtimxs it sxxms to mx that our txam is somxwhat likx an old typxwritxr - - not all of thx parts arx working propxrly. You may say to yoursxlf, "Wxll, I am only onx pxrson. I won't makx or brxak an organization." But, it doxs makx a diffxrxncx bxcausx a group, to bx xffxctvx, nxxds activx participation of xvxry singlx pxrson. So thx nxxt timx you think you arx only onx pxrson, and that your xfforts arx not nxxdxd, rxmxmbxr my old typxwritxr, and say to yoursxlf, "I am a kxy pxrson on this txam and I am nxxdxd vxry much."

Ole and Lena

Ole happened to be out of town when it was his and Lena's wedding anniversary, so he sent her a check for a million kisses. Lena, annoyed at her husband's cheapness, sent back a card saying, "<u>Tanks for the anniversary check. Da mailman cashed it in for me dis morning.</u>"

Lena was driving down the freeway at 75 miles an hour, when suddenly the brakes failed. Lena screamed at Ole, "Vat should I do? Vat should I do?" Ole replied, "<u>Hit something cheap.</u>"

Ole noticed his friend Sven walking down the street with a lantern in his hand. Ole asked, "Vhere are you going with dat lantern?" "I'm going courting," Sven answered. "Courting?" Ole snorted. "I didn't carry no lantern when I vent courting." Sven replied, "<u>And look what you got.</u>"

Ole was jumped by two muggers and fought back hard, but was finally subdued. His attackers then proceeded to go through his pockets. "You mean you fought like that for 57 cents?" asked one of the muggers. "Is that all you wanted?" moaned Ole. "<u>I thought you were after the $400 in my shoe!</u>"

Ole sat in the doctor's office muttering, "I hope I'm sick . . . I hope I'm sick." Lars overheard him and said, "Ole, vhy do you vish you vere sick?" Ole said, "<u>Vell, I'd hate to feel dis rotten if I vas vell.</u>"

Ole was hunting big game in Africa when he suddenly came screaming through the jungle. "What's the matter?" asked the guide. "A lion bit off my big toe," said Ole. "Which one?" asked the guide. "<u>How vould I know?</u> said Ole, "<u>Dose lions all look da same to me!</u>"

Did you hear about the intelligent Norwegian? It was just a rumor.

What's the best thing to come out of Norway lately? An empty boat.

Angel

Ole said, "I call my wife Lena an angel because she is always up in the air harping about something."

Money

Ole said, "If I can't take my money with me when I die, I am not going."

Ole and the Doctor

Ole went to the doctor for a checkup. The doctor pronounced him fit as a fiddle for a man of 75 years. "How old was your father when he died?" inquired the doctor.

"Who says he's dead?" answered Ole. "He's 95 and in terrific shape. He rides a bike and golfs every day."

"Remarkable," commented the doctor. "How old was HIS father when he died?"

"Who says he's dead?" said Ole. "He's 120 years old and really in fantastic shape. Swims every day and goes bowling and runs uphill 10 miles every day. In fact, he's getting married next week."

"Why in the world would a man of 120 years of age WANT to get married?" asked the doctor.

"Who says he WANTS to?" Ole answered.

Were You Hurt?

Ole said to Lena, "Were you hurt?" Lena said, "What do you mean?" Ole said, "When you fell from Heaven?"

Better Cook
Lena got to be a better cook after she found out that the smoke alarm wasn't the timer!

Was It You?
Ole said to Sven, "Was it you that died or was it your brother?"

He Doesn't Know
Ole lent Sven $20,000 for plastic surgery and now he doesn't know what he looks like.

Ring
Ole said to Sven, "Your wedding ring is on the wrong finger." Sven answered, "I married the wrong woman."

Gourmet Cook
I am a gourmet cook — I make great toast!

They Let It
What do they do in London, England when it rains? They let it rain.

I Love All My Relatives
I love all my relatives on both sides. Unfortunately, I can't tell you about all of them because this book would be about 400 pages long.

Raising Teenagers
Raising teenagers is like nailing Jell-O to a tree.

Jimmy Hoffa
They just found Jimmy Hoffa – in the telephone book yellow pages under "cement."

New Exercise
I lie on the floor and cough to music.

Lost
I never get lost because everyone tells me where to go.

Blood Test
I can't talk right now since I have to study for a test. I am taking a blood test tomorrow.

Lithuania, Latvia and Estonia
In 2006, I went to Lithuania, Latvia and Estonia with Carl and Leona Stapel. Chris and Cheryl Quello retired from First English Church in Appleton and then went to Lithuania to be a minister for two years. We went and heard Chris' sermon and it was great. We went to their apartment. The next night I told 20 minutes of Ole and Lena jokes to the top ten Norwegian ministers from Norway and their wives, the ambassador from Norway to Lithuania and his wife, the assistant to the Bishop and his wife as well as our group. My jokes went over very well.

Jerry at the Hill of Crosses in Latvia where there are over one million crosses.

Gerry Stenson
Gerry is my nephew from St. Cloud, Minnesota. He did my CD of the best talk I have given in 60 years, so far. It was July 26, 2006 at our Midwest region meeting in Detroit, Michigan. There were 600 CUTCO managers and sales representatives that heard my talk. I was supposed to talk 25 minutes and instead I only talked for 24 minutes — 20 minutes of actual speaking and four minutes of laughing. I told my wife Donna that I invested over 30

hours preparing for this. She told me that it was more than 40 hours. Since many of the managers and sales representatives had not slept much the night before, I also had to wake them up and I did. This CD is now a collector's item. If you have one you should hang on to it.

The Harold and Mary Pettersen Story
Harold was a Rotary Group Study Exchange team leader from Lillehammer, Norway who came to Appleton. He was an exceptional team leader. Since he is Norwegian, it goes without saying.

The first time I met Harold, I told him I was 200% Norwegian. My father Norval was 100% Norsk and my mother Clara was 100% Norsk. That is 200%, isn't it?

I stayed with Harold and Mary when we were in Lillehammer, Norway. They were great hosts.

The Villa Phoenix Story
The Villa Phoenix and Klister House is a halfway house for adult men that have been on drugs, alcohol or both and are trying to get back into society. A friend of mine, Dan Rorabeck, invited me to a board meeting 22 years ago. This meeting was supposed to start at 7:00 p.m. but did not start until 7:45 p.m.

They invited me to the next board meeting and I told them that I would attend but that I would not be there until 7:45 p.m. They asked me why. I told them it was because they start their meetings 45 minutes late. After that, the board meetings started on time.

I have been the president of Villa Phoenix Board of Directors for about 13 years. We have a great board: Director Steve Hinton, Lisa Bouwer Hansen, Bill Lueck, Jim Hietpas and me. They tease me about our short monthly meetings since they last only 45-50 minutes. Never go blah, blah, blah when blah is plenty.

A couple of years ago, I told Steve that I hope he never quits. Steve put out his hand and said to me, "I won't quit if you don't." This board does a lot of good so I am not going to quit. Steve is great at his job. If everyone did their job as well as Steve does there would be every few problems in this world. Steve also has a wonderful wife, Lauren.

Never Quit

When you are wrestling with a gorilla, do not quit when you get discouraged. Do not quit until the gorilla gets discouraged.

My Father's Advice

If you are late to meet someone, you are telling him or her that his or her time is not important to you. Being late is a bad habit.

SCORE

I have belonged to SCORE (Service Corps of Retired Executives) for about 10 years. I was president about six years ago. Chuck Lewis sponsored me into SCORE and I sponsored him into Rotary. Gene Jessup, a young friend of mine (he's either 82 or 62), was the president during 2006-2007. I have learned a lot from Gene — some of it I tried to forget.

Two Great Doctors

We have had two great doctors — Dr. Hugh Hamel and Dr. Jack Anderson. I met Hugh and Arleigh Hamel in 1954 when we called on them shortly after they moved to Appleton. Bernice and I asked them to become members of Trinity Lutheran Church and they did. Dr. Anderson is the son of a great doctor. Both Hugh and Jack have a lot of compassion.

How Can That Be?

Our daughters came to Appleton for my 80th birthday (August 7, 2006). I had an appointment with Dr. Anderson for a checkup. Our daughter Toni asked if she could come with me. I said, "Of course you can." After the examination was over, Dr. Anderson said, "Jerry, there is nothing wrong with you." Toni said, "How can that be? He does not eat right and he does not exercise." I explained to Toni that I was Norwegian, I have a positive attitude, I have faith like my mother, I have a great sense of humor and can laugh at myself and my relatives lived to be old. Toni replied, "Dad, you are a medical miracle." I would have given $1,000 for a picture of Toni when Dr. Anderson said that there was nothing wrong with me. I went from "how can that be" to being a "medical miracle" in five minutes.

Birthday Prayer
Today, dear Lord, I am 80 and there's much I haven't done.
I hope, dear Lord, you'll let me live until I'm 81.
But then if I haven't finished all I want to do,
Would you let me stay a while until I'm 82?
So many places I want to go, so very much to see —
Do you think you could manage to make it 83?
The world is changing fast, there is so much in store
I'd like it very much to live until I'm 84.
And if by then I'm still alive I'd like to stay till 85.
More planes will be up in the air so I'd really like to stick around
And see what happens to the world when I'm 86.
I know, dear Lord, it's much to ask and it must be nice in heaven
But I would really like to stay until I'm 87.
I know by then I won't be fast and sometimes will be late
But it would be so pleasant to be around at 88.
I will have seen so many things and had a wonderful time
So, I'm sure that I'll be willing to leave at 89 — maybe.

The Harry and Jerry Show
At our Starbuck High School reunion ten years ago, Harry Erickson and yours truly told Ole and Lena stories for 30 minutes. Our classmates liked it so much that they asked us back five years later. Of course, it did not hurt that we worked cheap. In fact, free.

I Laughed So Hard My Face Hurt
The night before "The Harry and Jerry Show" ten years ago 12 of us got together and told jokes for two hours. I laughed so hard my face hurt. Most people you and I know have never laughed that hard.

Walter Larson, who was in charge of our high school reunion, called me about a month before we were supposed to again do 30 minutes of Ole and Lena jokes and told me that I'd better call Harry because he did not want to do it. I called Harry and said, "What do you mean you do not want to do the 'Harry and Jerry

Show'?" Harry explained that he couldn't remember anymore. I told him that he should write it down. The reason <u>we called it the "Harry and Jerry Show" instead of the "Jerry and Harry Show" was that it was the only way I could get him to do it.</u>

1945 graduates - Harry Erickson, Dick Schroeder, Walt Larson, Dick Peterson and Jerry

Jerry and the "Harry and Jerry Show" Dick Peterson and Jerry.

<u>Harry Erickson has the best sense of humor of anyone I have ever known. I laughed more at Harry's jokes and he laughed more at my jokes than anyone in the audience except Connie Brunkow from Chokio, Minnesota. Connie is the best laugher I have ever known. If you are fortunate enough to have gotten the DVD of the "Harry and Jerry Show" you can hear this beautiful young blonde that laughed more than anyone else in the audience. That was Connie. She is very special. The DVD is now a collector's item. Harry is married to Ada. She is a great wife.</u>

Only One
I am the only person I know that does not own a computer. I did get a radio last week and I really like it.

I Did Not
I did not realize what an interesting life I had until I started writing this book and the best is yet to come! Live your dream. I did. Wow!

Failure
Food for thought — Failure should be our teacher, not our undertaker. Failure is delay, not defeat. It is a temporary detour, not a dead-end street.

Lutefisk
Lefse and lutefisk are often served together. Lutefisk is cod that has been preserved in the traditional Norwegian way of soaking it in lye. The more you chew lutefisk the bigger it gets. It is definitely an acquired taste.

Just Learned
I "yust" learned to say "yelly" and then they changed it to "yam."

Try Not to Be
Try not to be jealous. We can't all be Norwegian.

How I Got My Start
People ask me how I got my start in life. My dad gave me one dollar then he took the dollar back. Afterwards he gave me a kick in the hind end and said, "Go get 'em, son." That's about what happened.

Things I got from my father: sense of humor, likeability and a great work ethic. My father gave me a lot. I learned all this by example. I'd rather see a sermon than hear one any day!

My Favorite Smart Aleck
My friend Bill Ure from Evanston, Illinois is my favorite smart aleck of all time. Bill's wife, Jackie, is sensational. I took care of Bill on two of Carl and Leona Stapel's trips: Middle Europe and Lithuania, Latvia and Estonia. We saw the Hill of Crosses in Lat-

via, a few feet from the Estonia border. There are over 1 million crosses and more are added every day. My father taught me that you never kid anyone you don't like. In Bill's case I'll make an exception. Jackie should wear medals since she must be a saint.

Life Is Good
Everything is coming up roses.

Trust Everyone, Then Check
I ordered five hundred red, white and blue ballpoint pens with my name, address and telephone number on every pen to give to my customers. When the pens came, <u>I counted them and found they had only sent four hundred eighty eight pens. I called the company and they did not even say they were sorry for the error. I do not know if they did in on purpose or not. They did send me the twelve pens but I never ordered from this company again. Twelve pens times one million orders is 12 million pens.</u>

Crime Does Not Pay
Crime does not pay — unless you are elected.

First Class
If you do not go first class, your children will.

Norwegians
• What is two miles long and has an IQ of six?
A Sons of Norway parade.
• There is a new Norwegian parachute.
It opens on impact.
• Why don't Norwegians want to play hide and seek?
Because no one wants to look for them.

Growing Up
Growing up poor is something money won't buy.

Hard Work
Opportunities are usually disguised as hard work. That's why many people don't recognize them.

New Diet
I have been on this new diet where I eat only vegetables and drink wine. I lost ten pounds and my driver's license. I never met a meal I didn't like. Do not get fat, it is overrated.

Magnificent Body
I have a magnificent body because I exercise. I fill the bathtub full of water, pull the plug then fight the current. Try it sometime. You will like it. Someone said to me, "Jerry, you are looking good. Have you been sick?"

Exercise
I get enough exercise just pushing my luck.

Jerry Otteson
I just got lost in thought. It was unfamiliar territory.

You Go First
Change is good. You go first!

Shirt for Christmas
I got a shirt from one of our daughters for Christmas. It said, "They tell me that I have the body of a God. Too bad it is Buddha."

We Are Worth a Fortune
Remember, old folks are worth a fortune –
Silver in their hair, gold in their teeth,
Stones in their kidneys, lead in their feet, and gas in their stomachs.
I have become a little older since I saw you last,
and a few changes have come into my life since then.

Frankly, I have become quite frivolous old gal.
I'm seeing five gentlemen every day.
As soon as I wake up, Will Power helps me get out of bed.
Then I go see John. Then Charlie Horse comes along,
When he is here, he takes all my time and attention.
When he leaves, Arthur Ritis shows up and stays the rest of the day.

He doesn't like to stay in one place very long,
so he takes me from joint to joint.
After such a busy day, I'm really tired and glad to go to bed with
Ben Gay. What a life …

P.S. The preacher came to call the other day.
He said at my age, I should be thinking about the hereafter.
I told him I do all the time.
No matter where I am — in the parlor, upstairs,
in the kitchen, or down in the basement – I ask myself,
"<u>Now what am I here after?</u>"

I'm Fine
I'm fine, I'm fine.
There's nothing whatever the matter with me.
I'm just as healthy as I can be.
My pulse is weak and my blood is thin,
But I'm awfully well for the shape I'm in.

My teeth will eventually have to come out,
And I can't hear a word unless you shout.
I'm overweight and I can't get thin,
But I'm awfully well for the shape I'm in.

My memory is bad and I have blackouts,
And I keep alive on pills, no doubt.
I can't remember just where I've been,
But I'm awfully well for the shape I'm in.

I have heart failure and valves that leak,
And neuropathy causes my legs to be weak.
To tell you more would just be a sin,
'Cause I'm awfully well for the shape I'm in.

The moral is, as this tale unfolds,
That for you and me who are growing old,
It's better to say, "I'm fine" with a grin,
Than to let people know the shape we're in.

Older I Get

The older I get, the better I was. I am so old that my social security number is two. Moses is 1. I am older than dirt. When I order a three-minute egg, they make me pay in advance. Some people say, "Who would want to be 90?" And I say, "Anyone who is 89."

My Get Up and Go Has Gone Up and Went

How do I know that my youth is all spent?
Well, my get up and go has got and went.
But in spite of it all, I am able to grin
When I recall where my get up has been.

Old age is golden, so I've heard said,
But sometimes I wonder when I get into bed
With my ears in the drawer and my teeth in a cup
My eyes on the table until I wake up.

Ere sleep dims my eyes I say to myself,
Is there anything else I should lay on the shelf?
And I'm happy to say as I close the door,
My friends are the same, perhaps even more.

When I was young, my slippers were red,
I could kick up my heels right over my head.
When I grew older my slippers were blue
But still I could dance the whole night through.

Now I am old my slippers are black,
I walk to the store and puff my way back.
The reason I know my youth is all spent
My get up and go has got up and went.

But I really don't mind when I think with a grin
Of all the grand places my get up has been.
Since I have retired from life's competition
I busy myself with complete repetition.

I get up each morning, dust off my wits,
Pick up the paper and read the "obits."
If my name is missing, I know I'm not dead,
So I eat a good breakfast and go back to bed.

Aging
Some people try to turn back their odometers. Not me, I want people to know why I look this way; I've traveled a long way and some of the roads weren't paved.

Redneck
If you refer to fifth grade as your graduation, you might be a redneck.

Draft
Why doesn't the Norwegian government draft anyone for the Army until they are 45? It is because they want them to finish high school first.

Norwegians
There are two kinds of people in the world: Norwegians and those that want to be Norwegians. There are a lot of "wanna be's." Thank God I am Norwegian. Improve your image — be seen with a Norwegian.

Why?
Why do Norwegians like lightning? It is because they think they are having their picture taken.

Hard to See
It is hard to see the future when you have tears in your eyes.

Win or Lose
You can choose to either win or lose. So win!

Jokes
All my jokes are Norwegian because I am 200% Norsk so no one can get upset with me when I tell a Norwegian joke.

Memory
I have a memory like a steel trap. The only problem is that my steel trap memory sometimes gets rusty. An old Norwegian philosopher said that if your memory starts to slip, forget it. I do this many times a day. Old age is not for sissies.

Good Day
Dear God:
So far it's been a good day -
I haven't yelled, I haven't spat.
I haven't gossiped or kicked the cat.
I haven't whined or fussed.
But great the task that lies ahead,
For now I must get out of bed.
Amen.

Lance Armstrong
Lance Armstrong was told he had a 3% chance of living. Even though it was only 3%, he never gave up. He said that there were two kinds of days: good days and great days. The worst day he has is a good day. When you and I think this way, we will automatically be happier and live longer. Let's live longer!

Refrigerator Magnets
I collect refrigerator magnets. When I was in Amsterdam, the home of Anne Frank, I asked all the magnet vendors if they had any Anne Frank magnets. The vendors asked who Anne Frank was, which was surprising since we were two blocks away from where she had lived.

Best Thing
The best thing you can do for your children is to teach them by example, think positive and to believe in themselves. It is also important that you love their mother.

Think Positive!
If you want to get somewhere, you have to know where you want to go and how to get there. Then never, never, give up.

The secret to life isn't in what happens to you, but what you do with what happens to you.

Help other people to cope with their problems and your own will be easier to cope with.

Never use the word *impossible* seriously again. Toss it into the verbal wastebasket.

Self-trust is the first secret of success. So believe in and trust yourself.

Stand up to your obstacles and do something about them. You will find that they haven't half the strength you think they have. Joy increases as your give it, and diminishes as you try to keep it for yourself. In giving it, you will accumulate a deposit of joy greater than you ever believed possible.

How you think about a problem is more important than the problem itself – so always think positively.

Go at life with abandon; give it all you've got. And life will give all it has to you.

Expect People
If you expect people to like you, most of them will.

Al Miller and John and Lucille Peterson
Al, John and Lucille drove to Appleton from the LaCrosse area and stayed with me for the weekend. We played 500 (great card game) for 12 hours on Friday. Al and I played against John and Lucille. On Saturday morning, we played a new card game (for me). The others had played this game for more than 40 years. I won the first two games.

When anyone comes to see me, they get the opportunity to wash and dry my dishes. <u>I need all the help I can get!</u>

My Trip With Ken Schmidt
My second CUTCO son, Ken Schmidt from Houston, Texas, flew to Appleton on September 5, 2007. He stayed at my home overnight and on Thursday morning, we drove to Plymouth, Minnesota. Since Highway 10 was moved, we were delayed 45 minutes. (Ask Ken Schmidt for his version of this.) We stayed overnight with Denny, my third CUTCO son, and Mary Mahoney. It was Mary's 29th birthday and Denny took all four of us out to dinner. Denny is very fortunate to have a great wife like Mary.

On Friday morning, Ken and I drove to my hometown — Starbuck, Minnesota. We went to the Starbuck Card Room. My second cousin, Larry Kittleson and I played the World Champion Whist Players. They play whist as partners ten hours a day and eight hours on Sunday. Dick Engbretson, Dick Feigum and Larry Kittleson made no mistakes. Even though I made mistakes we won all but two games. You may ask how many games we played. The answer is three. This was one of the many highlights of our trip.

The Starbuck Card Shop

That night I invited fifteen of my relatives, friends and high school classmates to dinner. It was wonderful. We laughed for three hours.

After visiting the Corn Palace, we drove to Wall Drug Store in Wall, South Dakota. Wall Drug started in 1931 in the heart of the biggest depression in the history of the United States. Only 850 people currently live in Wall. A cup of coffee costs 5¢. Ken took a picture of my younger cousin and me at Wall Drug (next page).

Playing whist at Starbuck card shop

The Badlands were unbelievable. Our timing to see them was perfect. If we had been 20 minutes later, it would have been dark part of the time. If we had been an hour earlier, it would not have been as good. It pays to live right. The clouds, sun and rainbow made it just beautiful. I will never forget this 30-mile loop going through the Badlands. Ken made me buy a picture of the Badlands. Every time I look at this picture, I will think about this trip. My friend Dennis Vorpahl will frame it for me.

During our trip, we had perfect weather except for the day we went to Mount Rushmore. It rained so hard that we saw Noah twice. It only rained twice that day — once for 10 hours and another time for 14 hours.

The Crazy Horse head carving is bigger than all four of the Presidents put together at Mount Rushmore. The horse in this carving is much, much bigger than Crazy Horse. It will be many, many years until the horse is finished. We drove through Custer State Park. You need to drive very slowly because the road is narrow and cars are coming down the same road on the other side. One of the biggest bull buffalos I have ever seen walked across the road and was within a few inches of our car. We saw many herds. There are about 1,300 buffalos in the park. We probably saw half of them. When the bull buffalo is two and a half years old, they are culled out because they become violent and people could be in danger. They make buffalo burgers and ribs from them. I had buffalo ribs, the best I have ever had. No fat.

Don Lund, my Donna and me at Riverview County Club

What kind of shirt was Custer wearing when he died? An Arrow shirt.

Tanya Walter
Tanya is our granddaughter. Tanya stayed with Donna and me every Friday from age 5 to 7. Her mother asked me to buy Tanya a pair of boots. The boots Tanya wanted were awful. The ones I wanted were great. I told her that it was either these or none. Tanya said, "<u>I'll take these.</u>" She told her mother this the day after we bought the boots.

Tanya's Wise Sayings:
1. June 22, 1986 – I was whispering secrets in Tanya's year and I said, "I love you, Tanya." Tanya said, "<u>Grandpa, that's no secret, everyone knows that.</u>"
2. Tanya said, "Anyone who knows me loves me." Wouldn't it be wonderful if everyone felt that good about themselves? I told Tanya every day how great she is. My dad and mother told me every day how great I was and how much greater I was going to be.
3. Tanya and her mother were sitting with Donna and I and she said to me, "Grandpa, you have a staring problem." (I was looking at her.)
4. A customer brought her broken trimmer to me (it had been misused) and I replaced it for her free. When the customer left, Tanya told her, "Don't break this one, lady."
5. Tanya told Donna, "I don't think President Reagan can be

at my mother's wedding."
6. Tanya asked Donna, "Did grandpa really say, "I can hardly wait until Friday when Tanya comes here."
7. Tanya was here the other day for a few minutes and she was up in the kitchen with Donna when this customer came to see me. Tanya ran down to my office like she was shot out of a cannon. She likes to watch me when customers come to see me. As soon as this customer left, Tanya said to me, "Grandpa where is the sharpener?" I did not realize that I had sold my last sharpener to the last customer that had been there. Tanya is a very special little girl.
8. Donna asked Tanya, "What is a grandpa?" "He eats and he doesn't work."
9. "President Reagan is coming home from the hospital – the weather man said so."
10. Tanya said to me, "Grandpa, we have a situation here."
11. "Grandpa, I won't be crabby at the dentist. I had a nap."
12. Tanya said to Donna, "I have to whisper ain't because grandpa said I can't say ain't."
13. Tanya told Donna and me, "They don't sell cats in Neenah." That is what Tanya was told by Pat when she wanted them to get a cat. (Pat is Tanya's mother.)
14. I asked Tanya if she wanted to be a nurse. She said, "Grandpa, little kids can't be nurses."
15. I called Pat and asked her, "Can Tanya come over and play?"
16. Tanya would ask me every time she was here, "Let's play sell grandpa."
17. Tanya told Donna, "I want to be a mother. I hate being a kid."
18. I asked Tanya what she liked best about our trip to North Dakota and Minnesota. She said, "Seeing great grandma Otteson and Cameron."
19. Tanya told a customer that came to see me, "I'm putting Norwegian hand cream on my feet to make them better."
20. Tanya said to Donna, "Shall I tell you how my life is going?"
21. I was driving a rental car while our car was being serviced. I was not used to this car and it was raining hard and I did

not know how to turn on the windshield wipers. Tanya was sitting in the back seat in a seatbelt. Donna was yelling at me that she could not see as we were driving. Tanya said, "I want to come up to the front seat with you grandma so I can see how well grandpa is driving."

22. Tanya asked me, "Why is it when I ask you for something you always say, we'll see and we'll see means no?" Tanya was 6.

Tanya's Story

Below is a short story our 15-year-old granddaughter Tanya Walter wrote for her English class. There will always be a special place in my heart for Tanya. She spent every Friday with us for three years. It started when she was five years old and continued until she was seven. Her short story had to be short so she did not put in her story that I always set up two CUTCO service calls in our office in our home. Tanya watched me do 150-200 service calls in the three years. After the customer had left, Tanya would always ask me, "Can we play customer now?" First she would be the salesperson and I would be the customer. Next she would be the customer and I would be the salesperson. Tanya saw more CUTCO service calls than 95% of CUTCO managers.

We all remember certain things from our childhood that make us light up with happiness when we think about them. One such time for me was the Fridays I spent with my grandparents.

Early in the morning while I was still sound asleep, my mother would take me, all bundled in my pajamas, and place me in our car. She would then take me to my grandma and grandpa's house on the north side of Appleton. When I think about the memories, I can still feel every detail.

First, I remember the crisp morning air as I stepped from the car and walked the distance to the cement steps leading to the front door. Next, I can remember opening the door to the most fun place I had ever been. Upon entering the house and walking down the hall and up the staircase to the kitchen, I can still clearly envision my grandmother. Every Friday, it was the same picture. There she would sit, in her nightgown and housecoat, eating toast that was dark brown, drinking her plain black coffee, and watching the

Today Show. I could never understand why she liked that show. I much preferred to retreat to her living room and watch cartoons in solitude.

After watching several cartoons, my grandmother would call for me to come in the kitchen and eat some breakfast. To this day, I can still taste what was to come. I know immediately that my breakfast would contain wheat toast that was lightly browned, spread with butter and topped with cinnamon and sugar. The toast would be accompanied by a small mug filled halfway with black coffee. My mother had repeatedly told my grandmother that I was not to be given coffee, but she did not seem to hear my mother.

Upon finishing my breakfast, I always asked the same question, "Can I wake up Grandpa now?" Sometimes, if I was lucky, she would say yes. I still remember the giddy feeling that I would get in my stomach. Much the same feeling as when a boy asks you on a date. If my request was granted, I would bound up the carpeted stairs and run the short hallway to my grandparents' room. I would slowly open the door and carefully tiptoe across their carpeted floor. When I would reach the large bed in which my grandfather was sleeping, I would take a deep breath and let out a small giggle. As a smile crossed my face, I would leap onto the bed and jump around, yelling, "Wake up, Grandpa," in an almost taunting voice. I am not sure he enjoyed this practice, but he was never upset if I woke him up.

After my grandfather finally got out of bed, and everyone was dressed, he would announce that he had to run some errands. Every Friday, he would then ask me if I wanted to go along with him. Every Friday, my little voice would happily answer him with a yes. I knew where we would be going. The errands were always the same. Our first destination would be the car wash. My grandfather is a firm believer that a car should be washed once a week. I did not mind this belief because I was filled with joy to watch through the huge glass window that followed the car on the length of its journey. I loved watching the soap streams and rags that slapped at the car as it inched along on the tracks. The soapy bubbles that gathered on the floor always seemed to attract my attention and as I watched this great phenomenon I could smell the steamy water and soap as it wafted in to greet my nose. I still love the smell of a car wash and I think these memories are the reason why.

Our last destination would be the Shopko Plaza, now called the Northland Mall. _After walking a half-mile to the entrance because my grandpa wanted to park away from everyone to make sure no one hit his car,_ we could enter through the big double glass doors. I remember the smells that came our way as we entered. It was the smell of popcorn, buttery and salty. _My grandpa would always let me either choose a plain ice cream cone or a bag of popcorn, never both._ I can remember the taste of these delicious items as they filled my midmorning hunger attack. If I was having an extremely lucky day, there would be animals in the middle of the mall. _During my Friday experiences, I had the opportunity to ride on elephants, camels, and one time I was lucky enough to hold a baby lion. This was extremely special to me because I have a picture of me and the lion and I can still feel the soft fur of the fuzzy animal as I try to remember the event._

After the excitement of the popcorn or ice cream and the animals, we were ready to return home to my grandmother. Upon our arrival, we would find her busily cleaning the house in some way and the smell of cleaning products still comes to mind. Seeing our return, she would begin to make lunch. My lunch always consisted of a can of SpaghettiOs®, crackers and cheese, and apple slices. It would be delivered to me on a red and silver tray on the living room floor. I was then allowed to watch Sesame Street and Mr. Rogers.

Once lunch was devoured, I was told that I would have to take a nap. I willingly obeyed, tired out from the excitement of the day, and was allowed to nap on the couch.

As I would awake from my slumber, my mother would be there for the return to our home. She would always tell my grandmother that I was not supposed to be sleeping on the couch, but once again my grandma did not seem to hear her.

Today, my grandparents' home is still one of my favorite places to be and I will never forget those "special" Fridays spent with my two favorite people — my grandpa and grandma.

What Will Matter

Ready or not, some day it will all come to an end.
There will be no more sunrises, no days, or hours or minutes.
All the things you collected, whether treasured or
forgotten will pass to someone else.
Your wealth, fame and temporal power will shrivel to irrelevance.
It will not matter what you owned or what you were owed.
Your grudges, resentments, frustrations and
jealousies will finally disappear.
So, too your hopes, ambitions, plans and to-do lists will all expire.
The wins and losses that once seemed so important will fade
away.
It won't matter where you came from or
on what side of the tracks you lived.
It won't matter whether you were beautiful or brilliant.
Your gender, skin color, ethnicity will be irrelevant.
So what WILL matter?
How WILL the value of your days be measured?
What WILL matter?
Is not what you bought, but what you built;
not what you got, but what you gave.
What WILL matter is not your success, but your significance.
What WILL matter is not what your learned, but what you taught.
What WILL matter is not your competence, but your character.
What WILL matter is not how many people you knew,
but how many will feel a lasting loss when you're gone.
What WILL matter is how long you will be remembered,
by whom and for what.
Living a life that matters doesn't happen by accident.
It's not a matter of circumstance but of choice.
Choose to live a life that matters.

Donna Otteson

"My Donna" would have been 80 years old on October 23, 2007. That was a very hard day for me. My good friends Kris and Annelise Jensen called and took me out to dinner. It helped to be around good friends.

In Loving Memory of
Donna J. Otteson
Born to Life - October 23, 1927
Born to Eternal Life - June 13, 2007

When you're along with Jesus
And He sweetly smiles on thee,
Will you gently whisper to Him
A little prayer for me?
And when I'm along with Jesus
And all else is hid from view,
I'll gently drop into his heart
A little prayer for you.

Donna's Funeral

A few words from Donna's funeral that bless her memory:

Rev. Mary Beth Kovanen

Jesus said it simply . . . be yourself, say it as it is, be honest. It's a no-nonsense approach to life . . . and it helps me understand the impact Donna Otteson had on so many lives . . . Donna didn't try to be someone else. Donna was Donna. This is an incredible freedom in being yourself.

Donna didn't need to impress anyone. Donna had her own sense of what's right, her experience taught her the way things ought to be, or the way things could be. As part and parcel of her no-nonsense way of life . . . Donna could speak the truth when the truth needed telling . . . even if it caused a stir, or forced others to reckon with her. That didn't stop Donna from being Donna.

There are times in life when we need a good word . . . not a lengthy lecture, not a philosophical pondering, not even a wornout cliché. Today is such a day. I'll give it to you short and sweet: "Simply do justice, love kindness, and walk humbly with God." A good word.

<u>Donna Otteson was a good woman.</u> A woman who looked life in the eye, without blinking, and seemed to say, "Ah, what the heck. Let's make the best of it." And that's where her sense of devotion comes in. She went to work to make the best of it. At home she managed a household of seven girls and a traveling salesman husband. When the girls were teenagers and involved in all the things teens are involved in, Donna put 40,000 miles a year on the old Woody, the Ford Country Squire station wagon, without leaving the Fox Valley.

Here at Trinity, she let her deeds tell the story of her faith and devotion, helping coordinate funeral lunches for twelve years, serving as a communion assistant, Monday morning offering counter, hosting gatherings of the retirement group and simply showing up Sunday after Sunday. If you needed something done, Donna was ready to lend a hand. "Do justice, love kindness, walk humbly with God." Yeah, in Donna we see a glimpse of what that looks like.

"God did not give us a spirit of timidity" and Donna was not timid! I chose this verse to describe Donna's life because in her I saw that spirit, that spunkiness, that feistiness. She had a spirit of power, the way Donna carried herself, presented herself to the world. <u>She was a confident and capable woman.</u>

Donna did her best to live a life of faith with confidence even though it wasn't easy at times. The first day Kurt and I visited with Donna at Brewster Village, we asked her if she needed anything. She looked right at me and said, "<u>Yeah, why don't you spring me, help get me out of here.</u>" <u>That was her spirit of power showing through. After a few moments, she said, "Yeah, yeah, all right. Let me give you a tour of this place. It's really nice.</u>"

Over these last few months and perhaps years, it might have been easy for Donna to become depressed or angry. I'm sure Donna had these moments but she didn't have <u>only</u> those moments. Her courage and confidence helped her make the best of it.

"A cheerful heart is good medicine, but a downcast spirit dries up the bones." You might begin to wonder why this word fits Donna. Doesn't the word "humor" describe a person named Jerry? <u>Well, I have come to realize that only a person with a good sense of humor could ever marry Jerry Otteson.</u>

And the biggest surprise of all is that she might have been more humorous than he! Just a few weeks ago, Donna was talking with Brewster Village volunteer, Chaplain Pastor John McFadden, and he made a reference about someone but then he couldn't quite remember the person's name. Without blinking, <u>Donna looked up at him and said, "You call yourself a minister and yet you can't remember names?"</u>

During a dinner party at the Red Ox Supper Club last winter Kurt and I sat next to Donna and Jerry. Have you ever had that good fortune? It's happened to me a couple of times now and I'm getting to know the punch lines of Jerry's jokes so well that if he stumbles a bit I might just say it for him.

Jerry was in fine form that evening but Donna kept leaning over to us and whispering comments that were just as funny as Jerry. On one occasion, Jerry had just informed everyone of the best way to fall asleep if you ever have trouble falling asleep. Jerry said you just need to lie there in bed and imagine your mind is like a flooded basement and then pull the plug out of the drain and let everything in your mind go empty. Let everything simply go down the drain. <u>He claimed it works every time. And Donna leans over to us and says, "Just be careful you don't wet the bed."</u>

<u>Today is a day when we can celebrate the joy of having known Donna Otteson.</u> My friends, the kingdom of God is in our lives. The yeast of God's promising power is being experienced in our lives and it lifts us up. Like Donna's own life reveals, this is not a promise that bad things will not happen. Rather his promise as-

sures us that whatever does happen to us, whatever pain or problem may plague us, whatever fear may face us, whatever guilt may burden us, we are not alone.

Donna Otteson, wife, mother, grandma, sister, daughter, friend and child of God. She'll always hold a place in our hearts. For we know that nothing, not even death can separate us. The love of God binds us all together. Wherever we are, God is with us. When this world is at an end for us, God has another world in store for us. A world in which disappointment will vanish and joy will be forever. That's a promise. Thanks be to God. Amen.

Rev. Mary Beth Kovanen

This Is What Our Daughter Toni Said at Donna's Funeral
Our mom was tough. She was feisty. She was proud. She was proud of where she came from, her North Dakota farming roots, from a large, loving family with six brothers and sisters, all here today, and so many nieces and nephews. We are proud of who our mother became: a devoted wife, a loving mother, grandmother, great-grandmother and trusted friend. And she would be very proud today, having so many here to celebrate her life. Mom moved from North Dakota to Appleton 42 years ago with four kids in tow after finding love again. She made her life with Jerry, our dad, and seven daughters. She was proud of her new community and took active leadership in numerous church and civic roles and she also had fun! Mom helped Dad in his success and much of her life was devoted to his business, even making a few sales herself from time to time — pocketing in the cash, of course! Part of being a sales manager's wife meant participating in sales conventions and events. Mom excelled in this role and enjoyed the places and people she met, not to mention the new outfits she would need each time. She was elegant. It was from the inside, but a nice new outfit never hurts either.

Most of all, Mom was proud of her children. During the early years with kids at home, Mom was mostly on her own with nine mouths to feed. Dad had little choice but to work long and hard. But she could do it on her own! She was organized and decisive. No nonsense was allowed and unless you were bleeding badly, you were okay. She did a remarkable job, and she never put herself first. You may not have heard "I love you" but she showed it in her actions.

As kids were launched, Mom had more time for her involvements at the hospital auxiliary, church and local schools as well as her many bridge and book clubs. She had many friendships developed through these and other involvements that enriched her life so fully.

When grandchildren and then great-grandchildren came, it was a pleasure and joy for her. Visits were often busy times for Mom. She would bake and cook in preparation.

<u>Our mom was a great role model for her daughters and now we are feisty, proud and competent because of her. We thank you, Mom. You will be greatly missed but never forgotten.</u>

Her children aside and call her blessed — her husband also, and he praises her. Many women do noble things, but you surpass them all.

Al DiLeonardo

Al is the president of the eastern part of the United States for our company. Al and John Kane invited me to Philadelphia to speak to their staff. I was supposed to talk for 35 minutes but I talked for 30 minutes. If you want to be popular, talk less than they ask you to talk.

John Kane

John Kane met me at the Philadelphia airport on November 12, 2007. He then took me to Valley Forge. I was a history major and there is a lot of history at Valley Forge. We stayed with John and Tracy Kane for two nights and had dinner with John Kane's father, mother and younger sister. We then stayed with Al at his summer home on the shore. I have been around the world twice but had never been to Atlantic City.

Al took John and me to Atlantic City for a great dinner but the company was even better. We also walked on the boardwalk. They really gave me the red carpet treatment and I really appreciated it. Like all great men – Al has a wonderful wife. Al is a managers manager and is one of my favorite people.

It Is OK to Clap
When you are giving a talk and only a few are clapping, you say, "It is okay to clap. I have the time." If your timing is right the audience will laugh every time.

Oscar Boldt
Oscar Boldt gave a 30-minute talk in San Diego, California on ethics. There is no one I know that is more qualified to talk about ethics than Oscar Boldt. All of us are very proud of you Oscar.

Hugh Begy
Hugh Begy is my new friend from Rotary. He is a wonderful man. Hugh drove me to Starbuck, Minnesota on July 3, 4, 5, 2008 – all school reunion. We laughed full time.

In Memorial
Aunt Thelma Seldvig – Died at the age of 102. She was a wonderful aunt.

Rollie Tonnell
Rollie died about a year ago. Rollie was one of the best friends I ever had.

Dennis Vorpahl
Dennis was a true friend of "my Donna" and me for over 40 years. Dennis died of a massive heart attack at the age of 61. The last few months were his happiest because he met the love of his life, Cindy Brown. I met Cindy at the funeral and I can see why Dennis loved her.

Ken Johnston
Ken Johnston – Ken was my "Rotary" friend. He wrote a song for me entitled, "Skal to Jerry."

Jason Grall
Jason Grall - His wonderful wife was killed in a car accident.

I pray for all these people every day.

Tips for Managers

1. Spend at least 15 minutes each day handwriting thank-you notes.
2. Stand behind people in times of stress and crisis.
3. Treat others the way you want to be treated.
4. Return phone calls with dispatch.
5. Remember that change is a door that can only be opened in the inside.
6. Don't always look for the one right answer.
7. Dress for success.
8. Victory starts in your mind! Dream bigger!
9. Empower others. Be an enabler.
10. Improve your oral communication skills.
11. Praise in public. Criticize in private.
12. Carefully manage your time. It's your least renewable resource.
13. Be humble in victory and gracious in defeat.
14. Spell and pronounce names and titles correctly.
15. Have someone whom you may confide in.
16. Don't surround yourself with "yes" people.
17. Remember that success is getting up just one more than you fall down.
18. Know when to advance and when to retreat.
19. Don't ask someone to do something you wouldn't do yourself.
20. Remember, friends come and go, but enemies accumulate.
21. Be decisive. Avoid the ready, aim, aim, aim . . . syndrome.
22. Maintain an optimistic outlook.
23. Network with people outside of your field.
24. Be curious and openminded.
25. Schedule free or quiet time to think and plan without interruption.
26. Be an active listener.
27. Encourage and reward risk-taking. Have the courage to let go of the familiar.
28. Be a mentor to someone on the way up.
29. Be approachable.
30. Use "we" rather than "I" when talking about your firm.

31. Keep all promises. Don't promise more than you can deliver.
32. Strive for total quality/continuous improvement at all times.
33. Look at problems as opportunities.
34. Bring more humor into the workplace.
35. Recognize that consistently high performance may only be achieved if you take the time to recharge your batteries.
36. Use the K.I.S.S. principle (Keep It Simple Stupid) whenever possible.

Words to Live By
(Borrowed with pride by Jerry Otteson)

- Most demo's are too long. Be quick but do not hurry.
- As you go through life, you will have many opportunities to keep your mouth shut. Take advantage of all of them.
- Never say old to an old person.
- Nothing was ever achieved without enthusiasm.
- Ulcers are when you get from mountain climbing over molehills.
- Always try your best to make the most of the best and the least of the worst.
- Every single one of us has had our victories, so now when your troubles are the worst they've ever been and your stress is the hardest, look back on those good times for encouragement.
- The customer is always right – even when they are wrong.
- Happiness is something you decide on — ahead of time.
- The good news is that the bad news is not true.
- To avoid being a poor loser — win.
- Say to the customer before they bring out their favorite2-3 knives, "If you could see a wood handled knife under a microscope, you would never use that knife again – even for a minute."
- You can't spend money on Cutco - - you invest in Cutco.
- Count out loud enthusiastically when the customer cuts rope. Count both ways: 1, 2, 3, 4, 48, 49, 50.
- This is your paring knife. This is your trimmer. Assume it is

- going to be theirs.
- Cutco has feel appeal.
- Have every customer hold every piece of Cutco.
- The impossible is often within our reach.
- To be successful, it is 10% what happens to you and 90% how you handle it.
- Our Company is the best company in the world.
- Everyone needs Cutco.
- Nothing happens til you sell something.
- Cutco has quality written all over it.
- Always say only or just when you quote Cutco prices.
- Show 8 on Saturday. How do you show 8 on Saturday? Do what you did to show 4 but do it twice.
- Ask the Domestic Goddess to have her husband there when you get there. When she asks, "Why?", say "Because we need his opinion."
- Do not wait for opportunities, create them.
- If you can dream it, you can achieve it.
- Knowledge is power.
- Seven days without laughter makes you weak.
- Power P.C.'s are much better than P.C.'s.
- Common sense is not very common any more.
- Yesterday was the deadline for all complaints.
- He or she who angers you, controls you.
- There is no greater treasurer than a good friend.
- Life isn't about waiting for the storm to pass. It's learning to dance in the rain.
- It is easier to preach ten sermons than it is to live one.
- You can tell how big a person is by what it takes to discourage him/her.
- Peace starts with a smile.
- Some minds are like concrete . . . thoroughly mixed up and permanently set.
- If you didn't start your day with a smile, it's not too late to start practicing for tomorrow.
- I am an eternal optimist.
- Know how to prevent sagging? Just eat till the wrinkles fill out.
- Better to live rich than die rich.
- Smoked carp tastes just as good as smoked salmon when you

- don't have smoked salmon.
- When tempted to fight with fire, remember that the Fire Department usually uses water.
- Smile tricks the body into feeling great.
- Do not knock it until you try it.
- Accept the fact that some days you're the pigeon, and some days you're the statue.
- Always keep your words soft and sweet, just in case you have to eat them.
- Always read stuff that will make you look good if you die in the middle of it.
- If you lend someone $20 and never see that person again, it was probably worth it.
- Never put both feet in your mouth at the same time, because then you won't have a leg to stand on.
- Nobody cares if you can't dance well. Just get up and dance.
- Since it's the early worm that gets eaten by the bird, sleep late.
- The second mouse gets the cheese.
- Birthdays are good for you. The more you have, the longer you live.
- Some mistakes are too much fun to make only once.
- We could learn a lot from crayons. Some are sharp, some are pretty and some are dull. Some have weird names and all are different colors, but they all have to live in the same box.
- A truly happy person is one who can enjoy the scenery on a detour.
- Take a lot of vitamin F. F is for friends.
- Laugh like you mean it.
- No act of kindness, no matter how small, is ever wasted.
- Never underestimate the heart of a champion.
- May the rest of your years be the best of your years.
- Have a great week today.
- Never stop getting better.
- Enthusiasm is contagious. Let's start an epidemic.
- You don't have to win every agreement. Agree to disagree.
- Love your parents because they will be gone before you know it.
- Make peace with your past so it won't fowl up the present.
- It's OK to let your children watch you cry.
- Time heals almost everything. Give time time.

- Good is the enemy of great. This is not a business to be good at. This is a business to be great at.
- We do things that work so well, we stop doing it.
- It is okay to have talent, but 100% more important to have desire.
- Successful people do things failures refuse to do.
- When a customer says, "I would not use all those pieces," you say, "What <u>one</u> piece wouldn't you use?"
- There is not a right way to do the wrong thing.
- Do not get hardening of the attitudes.
- When they say they want a peeler, you say, "How many?"
- A kind word is like a spring day.
- A person that has a good sense of humor has nothing to fear from the world.
- I hear. I forget. I see. I remember. I do. I understand.
- It is never too late to have a great childhood.
- Treat every person like they are your mother.
- Everything you and I do is selling. Everything!
- Your attitude is more important then your aptitude.
- An optimist is a person who, when he wears out his shoes just figures he's back on his feet.
- The pessimist says, "I'll believe it when I see it." The optimist says, "I'll see it when I believe it."
- The optimist takes action and the pessimist takes a seat.
- Great works are performed not by strength but perseverance.
- Failure is success if we learn from it.
- No problem can stand the assault of sustained thinking.
- Hold yourself responsible to a higher standard then anyone else expects of you.
- No task will be evaded merely because it is impossible.
- Don't confuse activity with accomplishment.
- Success is not a destination; it's a journey.
- It is far better to attempt something great and fail, then it is to attempt nothing and succeed.
- You can get everything in life you want, if you help enough other people get when they want.
- As ye sow, so shall ye reap?
- When your self-image improves, your performance improves.
- Life is like a ladder, every step can take you either up or down.

- All sunshine makes a desert.
- What counts is not the number of hours you put in, but how much you put in the hours.
- Speak only if it is an improvement on silence.
- A man is like a tack; he can go as far as his head will let him.
- Forget the potholes in the road and celebrate the journey instead.
- Be a role model to someone.
- The man who tries to trim himself to suit everybody will soon whittle himself away.
- The bigger a man's head gets, the easier it is to fill his shoes.
- If you never stick your neck out you will never get your head above the crowd.
- Kites can only rise against the wind, not with it.
- The true art of memory is the art of attention.
- The trouble with stretching the truth is that it often snaps back.
- An open mind is fine but be careful what you shovel into it.
- It is easier to build a boy then to mend a man.
- You can't get anywhere today if you are still mired down in yesterday.
- You can't do anything about yesterday
- When your outgo exceeds your income, then your upkeep will be your downfall.
- Motivation is what gets you started. Good habits keep you going.
- Success is getting up one more time than you fall down.
- Never quit! You're a winner.
- Relax your body, not your efforts.
- Be kind to yourself. Look for improvement.
- You may have to fight a battle more than once to win it.
- Remember you are a worthy person who deserves to succeed.
- You are special.
- Refuse to accept missteps as failures. Try to identify the cause and learn from the experience.
- What you did is not important as what you learned from it.
- To go anywhere, you must begin. Let this be the first step of your journey.
- Nothing else ruins the truth like stretching it.
- The thing that counts is NOT what we could do, but what we

actually do.

- We have to learn how to win.
- If you need help, ask for it, if not prove it.
- Desire – is the most important word in the English language.
- You never stub your toe – unless you are moving forward.
- When you do your best, you feel your best.
- If all the sad words of tongue or pen, the saddest are these, "It might have been."
- The greatest ability you have is DEPENDABILITY.
- No one is in charge of your happiness but you.
- Frame every so-called disaster with these words, "In five years, will this matter?"
- However good or bad a situation is, it will change.
- Don't take yourself so seriously. No one else does.
- Believe in miracles.
- Don't audit life. Show up and make the most of it now.
- Growing old beats the alternative – dying young.
- Your children get only one childhood.
- All that truly matters in the end is that you loved.
- Get outside every day. Miracles are waiting everywhere.
- Envy is a waste of time. You already have all you need.
- The best is yet to come.
- Life isn't tied with a bow, but it's still a gift.
- Life is too short to waste time hating anyone.
- Your job won't take care of you when you are sick. Your friends and parents will. Stay in touch.
- Pay off your credit cards every month.
- Cry with someone. It's more healing than crying alone.
- Save for retirement starting with your first pay check.
- When it comes to chocolate, resistance is futile.
- Don't compare your life with others. You have no idea what their journey is all about.
- If a relationship has to be a secret, you shouldn't be in it.
- Everything can change in the blink of an eye. But don't worry; God never blinks.
- Get rid of anything that isn't useful, beautiful or joyful.
- It's never too late to have a happy childhood. But the second one is up to you and no one else.
- When it comes to going after what you love in life, don't take no for an answer.

- Today is special.
- Over prepare, then go with the flow.
- Motivation is what gets you started. Good habits keep you going.
- Success is getting up one more time than you fall down.
- Never quit! You're a winner.
- You don't have to throw a pass down the whole length of the field to score a touchdown. You can get there one yard at a time.
- What's in your mouth is not nearly as important as what is on your mind.
- What happened is in the past; what may happen tomorrow isn't for sure. Just change today.
- Be kind to yourself. Look for improvement.
- Life is like riding a bicycle. You don't fall off unless you stop pedaling.
- Be as good to yourself as you are to others.
- Remember you are a worthy person who deserves to succeed.
- You are special.
- Today, hug someone who has encouraged you.
- Refuse to accept missteps as failures. Try to identify the cause and learn from the experience.
- Do what you do best. If you are a runner, run. If you are a bell, ring.
- What you did is not important as what you learned from it.
- A Norwegian wanted to break a record for swimming across the English Channel. He swam half way across then got tired so he swam back.
- There is a new Norwegian parachute out – it opens on impact.
- People ask me if I was born in a log cabin. My answer is "no" but I moved to one as soon as we could afford it.
- I used to sleep til the crack of noon. Now I go to bed late and get up early.
- I was the valedictorian of my high school class. The other guy was not very bright.
- We moved to Fargo, North Dakota for the weather. That shows how smart we were.
- The latest dance craze? It is called the Politicians Polka. You take one step forward, two steps backwards and then side-

step the issue.

- Paul Harvey said, "When your memory fails – forget it."
- Never go blah, blah, blah when blah is plenty.
- Business is great, people are terrific, and life is wonderful.
- Life is not fair — GET USED TO IT.
- We can't do anything about yesterday, and many people spoil today by worrying about tomorrow.
- You only live once if you do it right, that is enough.
- The best way to prepare for tomorrow is to do today's work superbly.
- Attitude is everything.
- When our attitude is right the world is right.
- Repetition is the mother of skill.
- If it looks like a duck and if it quacks like a duck and if it has webbed feet — it is a duck.
- You attract what you are.
- Life is a journey. Enjoy the trip.
- Things we should all ask before we do anything:
    Is it safe?
    Is it legal?
    Is it moral?
    Does it make sense? And most importantly,
    Would my mother approve?
- The best baseball fans in the world are Chicago Cub fans . . . the Cubs are so bad this year, if you are one of the first nine to be at a home game, you get to start.
- A winner always finds a way.
- Two laws of stress reduction: Do not sweat the small stuff, and it's all small stuff.
- Never say: "Pretty excited." That translates to: "Half dead." Really excited is 100% better than pretty excited.
- Like the song says: "When you can't sleep, count your blessings instead of sheep."
- Praise can give criticism a lead around the first turn and still win the race.
- Make me feel good and I'll produce.
- We are on the elevator of opportunity.
- There is no limit to what you can do if you do not mind who gets the credit for it.
- We should develop an attitude of gratitude.
- If you think education is expensive, try ignorance.

- The older I get, the younger the old people are!
- Great salespeople never die; they just go out of commission.
- Temper always improves with non-use.
- Do not be frustrated — be fascinated!
- If you spend too much time looking in the mirror, it's easy to lose your balance.
- It is only when your feathers get ruffled that your true colors show.
- You can't build a reputation on what you're going to do.
- Do it now!
- Only the mediocre are always at their best.
- It's wonderful to grow old, if you remember to stay young while you're doing it.
- Talk about people's long comings — not their shortcomings.
- In school I was teacher's pet — she could not afford a dog.
- It's never too late to have a happy childhood.
- There are many nice things to be said about growing older — most of them are lies!
- Age is mind over matter — if you do not mind, it doesn't matter.
- Some people are making such thorough preparation for rainy days that they are not enjoying today's sunshine.
- I was really discouraged yesterday — I realized that half of my life is now over. How many 170-year-olds do you know? Jerry Otteson — age 85.
- We can handle any crisis — we have children!
- When selling ceases to be fun, selling ceases.
- Kids are like old people — with energy!
- Thinking is the hardest work there is, which is the probable reason why so few engage in it.
- There's always free cheese in a mousetrap.
- Think excitement, talk excitement, act out excitement and you are bound to become an exciting person.
- Happiness never decreases by being shared.
- Among those whom I like or admire, I can find no common denominator; but among those whom I love, I can: all of them make me laugh.
- Excellence is not an act but a habit. The things you do the most are things you will do best.
- The time is always right to do what is right.

- How to do something extraordinary . . .
  Stage #1: First it will seem impossible.
  Stage #2: Then it will become difficult.
  Stage #3: Finally, with persistence, it will get done.
- Laughter is a tranquilizer with no side effects.
- It takes 26 muscles to smile and 62 muscles to frown. Why not make it easy on yourself?
- Charm and wit and levity may help you at the start but at the end, it is brevity that wins the public's heart — Public Speaking Secret.
- People who have no faith in themselves seldom have faith in others.
- Ability is of little value without dependability.
- It takes less to keep an old customer satisfied than to get a new customer interested.
- Hardening of the attitudes is the most deadly disease on the face of the earth.
- Never let yesterday use up too much of today.
- Perhaps once in a hundred years a person may be ruined by excessive praise, but surely once every minute someone dies inside for lack of it.
- The key to willpower is a want power. People who want something badly enough can usually find the willpower to achieve it.
- The key to longevity: "Keep breathing."
- It is what we have learned after we know it all that counts.
- Why is it we never have time to do it right, but we always have time to do it over?
- If you do not like your lot in life, build on it.
- I was born at night, but it wasn't last night.
- Life breaks everyone, but some grow stronger at the broken places.
- After all is said and done, much more is said than done.
- Extravagance is the only luxury I will allow myself.
- Old Norwegian saying: "Leave the worrying to the horses because they have bigger heads."
- I am so excited that my goosebumps have goosebumps.
- Now that we know better, we can do it better.
- If you aim at nothing, you will hit it every time.
- It is hard to be humble when you're a Norwegian.

- The secret of happy living is not to do what you like, but to like what you do.
- A winner always finds a way.
- It is easier to give the customer service now than to take customer complaints later.
- A brilliant idea is a job half done.
- Expect to win. It is a funny thing about life; if you refuse to accept anything but the best, you usually get it.
- Well-organized ignorance often passes, unfortunately, for wisdom.
- All of us should have a Grateful Journal. We should enter things in this journal every day.
- Life can be either a celebration or a chore. The choice is up to you and me.
- Either you are part of the solution or you are part of the problem.
- Nothing to it but to do it.
- When the going gets tough, the tough get going.
- Nothing was ever achieved without enthusiasm.
- Everyone has a photographic memory. It's just that some people do not have any film.
- There is no strength where there is no struggle.
- Most of us know how to say nothing. Few of us know when.
- Your goals do not start in your brain; they start in your heart.
- Choose your words with taste. You may have to eat them someday.
- You can't make both ends meet sitting on one.
- Do not forget little acts of kindness, but do not remember little faults.
- Asking for trouble is a request that is seldom denied.
- Do the best you can, with what you have, where you are.
- Once a human mind is opened to a new idea, it never returns to its former dimensions.
- Learn from the mistakes of others. You can't live long enough to make them all yourself.
- The impossible is often within our reach.
- If you settle for less than you deserve, you will get even less than you settled for.
- Three simple questions to ask yourself when you are thinking of promoting someone:

Can they do it?
Will they do it?
Will they fit in?

- Our minds are like parachutes — they only do us good when open.
- The older I get, the better I was.
- E.I.G.T.B.O. — Everything is going to be okay.
- The really great person is the person who makes every person feel great.
- If you plant weeds, do not expect to pick flowers.
- You can't push a string — you can't motivate anyone if they do not want to be motivated.
- Blessed are those who give without remembering and take without forgetting.
- Be careful what you wish for . . . you might get it.
- I could not be happier if I was twins.
- You can't steal second base with one foot on first base. Go for it — take a chance. Go out on a limb — that is where the fruit is.
- A good example has twice the value of good advice.
- Three little words that are really BIG words: And then some.
- You can't motivate beyond their "Yearning Power."
- Always do what you say you are going to do.
- Failure should be our teacher, not our undertaker. Failure is delay not defeat. It is a temporary detour, not a dead end street.
- Success is merely a matter of luck — ask any failure.
- Laugh the loudest when the joke is on you.
- My favorite song of all time is:
  Accentuate the positive,
  Eliminate the negative,
  And do not mess with "Mr. In-Between."
- Rotary's Four Way Test is good for all of us:
  Is it the truth?
  Is it fair to all concerned?
  Will it build goodwill and better friendships?
  Will it be beneficial to all concerned?
- Most demos are too long.
- Most meetings are too long.
- You can not hold a person down without staying down with him or her.
- The three most important things in life — Attitude, Attitude,

Attitude.

- F.A.D. — Fun All Day. Have fun all day.
- You can't build a reputation on what you are going to do.
- The world's finest cutlery has CUTO written all over it.
- Every self-made person has a lot of working parts.
- I.A.S.O.C. — I am sold on CUTCO.
- Never borrow on tomorrow.
- Water under the bridge — that is the idea.
- Someday is not a day of the week.
- The world will not devote itself to making us happy.
- <u>I am on a constant wave of good fortune</u>.
- Every day I beat my own previous record of consecutive days I have stayed alive.
- People may not remember exactly what you said, or did, but they will always remember how you made them feel.
- Make me feel good and I will produce.
- High performers create their own opportunities.
- If your memory starts to slip — forget it. I do it many times a day.
- Never hold a $10,000 meeting to solve a $10 problem.
- Do not settle for good when you can be great.
- It is wonderful to grow old, if you remember to stay young while you are doing it.
- Seventy-six percent of people in the United States that have a bad attitude do not know they have a bad attitude.
- You do not stop laughing because you grow old. You grow old because you stop laughing.
- When your attitude is right, the world is right.
- The most important thing you can give someone is a chance.
- The best way to escape your problem is to solve it.
- I have learned that ultimately "takers" lose and "givers" win.
- The time is always right to do what is right.
- Quality never goes out of style.
- One person with a belief is more important than a thousand with just an interest.
- Nothing worthwhile is easy.
- If you can imagine it, you can achieve it. If you can dream it, you can become it.
- Enthusiasm is the yeast that raises the dough.
- You can't be a smart cookie with a crummy attitude.
- You are not born a winner or a loser. You are born a chooser.

- You are only as good as your product — and CUTCO is the best cutlery in the world.
- You are in the right place at the right time.
- Take life one nap at a time.
- When you do your best, you feel your best.
- Things turn out the best for people who make the best of the way things turn out.
- Your attitude always determines your altitude in this great business.
- On the day of victory, there is no fatigue.
- I am a CUTCO fanatic. We want you to be a CUTCO fanatic also.
- Welcome to the wonderful world of CUTCO.
- Anyone that knows all the answers has not been asked all the questions.
- No one ever says, "It's only a game," when their team is winning.
- It is not the customer's job to fire you up. It is your job to fire up the customer.
- I am happier than a woodpecker in a lumber yard. You can't be happier than that.
- It rained twice last week — once for four days and once for three days.
- If you are not selling now, you probably never did.
- We do many things now we do not get paid for, so later on we will get paid for many things we do not do.
- You will get everything you want in life; as long as you help others get what they want.
- Self esteem — Become your own best friend.
- People get jobs because of what they know; they lose them because of how they fit.
- If you do not know how to lose, you will never know how to win.
- Never laugh at anyone's dreams. People who do not have dreams do not have much.
- Do not follow anyone who is not going anywhere.
- I love my job, I love my job, I love my job, I love my job.
- I do not have to attend every argument I'm invited to.
- When all is said and done, much more is said than done.
- I'd rather be a failure at something I love than a success at

something I hate.
- Happiness is something you decide on ahead of time.
- The first rule of holes is when you are in one, stop digging.
- If you can't laugh at yourself, someone will do the job for you.
- The only person who can make you happy is you.
- You do not have to be a chicken to know a bad egg.
- Preparation makes you lucky. Does it ever.
- The reason dogs have so many friends is because they wag their tails, not their tongues.
- The only people you should get even with are those who helped you.
- Either you do it or you don't, but you do not try.
- The best way to make your dreams come true — is to wake up.
- A sincere compliment is the least expensive and most valuable gift you can give anyone.
- When you think positive, great things happen.
- Live as if you will die tomorrow, but dream as if you will live forever.
- If Appleton, Wisconsin is not heaven, it is in the same zip code.
- Everything turns out for the best — even when it does not seem so at the time.
- This is an exciting time to be alive.
- Good is the enemy of great.
- A big army always beats a small army.
- You will miss 100% of the shots (demos) you never make.
- Character is what you are when no one is looking.
- The road to success is always under construction.
- Success is largely a matter of hanging on after others have let go.
- Have a positive attitude about life, look for good, and find only good wherever you go.
- Do not find fault, find a remedy.
- The higher you climb, the harder the wind blows.
- The key to a good memory is to write everything down.
- Thoughts plus words plus action equals reality.
- It is not over until you win.
- If you do not believe in CUTCO, your believer is broken.
- CUTCO — where stars are born.
- I intend to live forever — so far, so good.
- Do not trust anyone whose stomach does not move when they

<u>laugh</u>.
- If you win a rat race, you are still a rat.
- Develop the skin of a rhino and the soul of an angel.
- If you see people without a smile today, give them one of yours.
- There is gold dust in the air.
- Even if you are on the right track, you will get run over if you just sit there.
- Ninety-nine percent of Norwegians give the rest a bad name.
- Eighty percent of life is showing up.
- You cannot laugh too much. If you laugh a lot, you will live longer.
- It is all about performance.
- A good exercise for the heart is to bend down and help another up.
- Happiness comes through doors you didn't even know you left open.
- Yesterday is history. Tomorrow is a mystery. Today is a gift. That's why its called: The Present.
- Pain and suffering are inevitable but misery is optional.
- Forgiveness does not change the past, but it does enlarge the future.
- Yesterday ended last night.
- Kids go where there is excitement. They stay where there is love.
- If people like you, they'll listen to you, but if they trust you they'll do business with you.
- Obstacles are the things we see then we take our eyes off our goals.
- Opportunity knocks but once, but temptation leans on the doorbell.
- Even if there is nothing to laugh about, laugh on credit.
- It is okay to fail. It is not okay to quit.
- The older I get . . . the more I have to learn.
- Learn to laugh at yourself. I do it every day!
- Be so good that people can't ignore you.
- You're one of a kind. Live with confidence.
- Have you complimented yourself lately?
- Do not go through life being against yourself.
- Dwell on your good traits.
- Grow to greatness.

- Be true to yourself.
- If you can breathe, you can lead.
- Pain is temporary; quitting is forever.
- If you fill your heart with regrets of yesterday and the worries of tomorrow, you have no today to be thankful for.
- You are richer today if you have laughed, given or forgiven.
- Anger is a condition in which the tongue works faster than the mind.
- You can't change the past, but you can ruin the present by worrying over the future.
- Love – and you shall be loved.
- All people smile in the same language.
- A hug is a great gift – one that fits all, it can be given for any occasion and it's easy to exchange.
- Happiness is something you decide on ahead of time.
- Don't live in the past. There is no future to it.
- Do not live worried.
- Do not close your heart.
- Laugh whenever you can.
- What you expect is what you get.
- Many people learn to listen but few listen to learn.
- Laugh at yourself.
- Bring joy wherever you go.
- Cheaters never win.
- To err is human, but when the eraser wears out before the pencil, you are overdoing it.
- There is no pillow as soft as a clear conscience.
- A dull knife is worse than no knife at all.
- Remember, growing older is mandatory. Growing up is optional.
- The person who knows everything has a lot to learn.
- It is easier to get to the top if you look like you belong there.
- There is no one that is so deaf as those that will not hear.
- There are three kinds of people in the world: those who can count and those who can't.
- This is not a business to be good at. It is a business to be great at.
- Be thankful every day.
- Selling "World Famous CUTCO Cutlery made in the good old USA" is like getting paid to eat ice cream.

- People won't go with you if they can't get along with you.
- You can't soar with the eagles if you cluck with the chickens.
- A problem well defined is half solved.
- You will never change what you tolerate.
- When you win, you can teach.
- I do not need new jokes, I need a new audience.
- If you live in the past, you will die in the past.
- You can't do it big 'til you dream it big.
- You will become what you think about most of the time.
- I crammed four years of college — into eight years.
- A person cannot live by bread alone. He must have peanut butter.
- Life is too short not to be a Norwegian.
- <u>If I have a single flower for each time I think of you, I could walk in my garden forever</u>.
- You may forget how you behaved when the going got tough, but others won't.
- If you are nice to people, you are already a success.
- There is no shortage of things to be excited about.
- You have to be all-day tough.
- Blessed are the flexible.
- No one has ever hurt his eyesight by looking at the bright side.
- What you did is not as important as what you learned from it.
- Motivation is what gets you started. Good habits keep you going.
- There are two kinds of people: those who help others and those who don't.
- You were born to win.
- Today's success was yesterday's decision. Tomorrow's success is today's decision.
- Success is not the key to happiness. Happiness is the key to success.
- Success is a choice.
- You can never get ahead by trying to get even.
- You can tell how big a person is by what it takes to discourage him/her.
- It is not about the knives, it's about the lives.
- Common sense is not very common anymore.
- You need to prepare your attitude ahead of time.
- Let us live so that when we die even the undertaker is sorry.

- Never look back unless you intend to go that way.
- If you do not know where you are going, any road will get you there.
- Do not ask the question if you cannot live with the answer.
- Never argue with an idiot. People watching may not be able to tell the difference.
- Make this the first day of the best of your life.
- Loyalty is almost a lost art.
- The heart that loves is always young.
- Inspire people to have confidence in themselves.
- You have what it takes to be great.
- Never wrestle with a pig. You both get dirty and the pig likes it.
- We can handle anything if we have the right attitude.
- Attitude is everything.
- The law of averages will always take care of you, if you give it a chance.
- A "Big Shot" is just a "Little Shot" that kept shooting.
- Quality never, never goes out of style.
- People with nothing to do want to do it with you.
- You do not have to be in Who's Who to know "what's what."
- It is your job and my job to make people feel good.
- We are in this world to help each other.
- Do not let what you cannot do interfere with what you can do.
- Humor is a great friend. Keep it close to you.
- People judge us by the way we talk . . . and they should.
- The most powerful four words in the English language are "I believe in you."
- Our customers have a choice: make sure it's us.
- Live like you mean it.
- The first thing you have to sell is not CUTCO. It is yourself.
- The person who knows how to laugh at himself will never cease to be amused.
- Laughing is a good exercise. It's like jogging on the inside.
- Kindness is like a boomerang. It always returns.
- You can't build a reputation on what you are going to do.
- The harder and smarter I work, the luckier I get.
- Every self-made person has a lot of working parts.
- No matter how well you are doing, you can do better.
- There are two types of fools: those who trust everyone, and those who trust no one.

- If you are serious about quality, call me.
- Every morning say to yourself, "Self, I'm healthy, I'm excited, and I'm great."
- Elephants and mistreated customers have long memories.
- Be the kind of person you want to attract.
- If you know how, you will always have a job. If you know why, you will be the boss.
- The truly great person is the one who gives you a chance.
- It is nice to be important, but it is more important to be nice.
- If someone says something unkind about you, live your life so no one believes it.
- An ounce of loyalty is worth a pound of cleverness.
- Faster than Jerry Otteson chasing an ice cream truck. . . Now that is fast.
- You never achieve real success until you love what you are doing.
- Ability can take you to the top, but it takes character to keep you there.
- Are you a blue ribbon optimist?
- When you lose your dreams, you die.
- People do business with people they like.
- Behave like a winner.
- When things go wrong, do not go with them.
- There is no such thing as a bad day. There are character building days.
- It is never too late to become what you might have been.
- How long has it been since you laughed so hard your face hurt?
- CUTCO keeps my life from getting dull.
- Compassion is difficult to give away because it keeps coming back.
- When you help someone up the hill, you are that much closer to the top yourself.
- CUTCO is the gift that keeps on giving.
- Enthusiasm is contagious. Let's start an epidemic.
- The customers are always right, even when they are wrong.
- When you have nothing to say, for heaven's sake say it!
- Life is a series of popularity contests.
- Few wishes come true by themselves.
- Enthusiasm rules the world. It always has and it always will.
- If you need help, ask for it — if not, prove it.

- Practice does not make perfect — perfect practice makes perfect.
- Desire is the most important word in the English language.
- R.I.T.M.O.A.L. — Repetition is the mother of all learning.
- A goal is a dream with a time limit
- Plan ahead — it wasn't even raining when Noah built the ark.
- When everyone wants a free ride, who will pull the wagon?
- You never stub your toe, unless you are moving forward.
- When you do your best, you feel your best.
- Of all the sad words of tongue or pen, the saddest are these, "It might have been."
- Yesterday is a canceled check. Tomorrow is a promissory note. Today is ready cash. Invest it wisely.
- In the big depression, fast food was when you ran over a chicken.
- How do you make a Norwegian laugh on Monday morning? Tell him joke on Wednesday afternoon.
- No one is in charge of your happiness except you.
- Frame every so-called disaster with these words: "In five years, will this matter?"
- Forgive everyone everything.
- Your job won't take care of you when you are sick. Your friends will. Stay in touch.
- Believe in miracles.
- Your children get only one childhood. Make it memorable.
- If we all threw our problems in a pile and saw everyone else's, we'd grab ours back.
- All that truly matters in the end is that you loved.
- Life is wonderful. It always has been. It always will be.
- Whenever you are asked if you can do a job, tell them, "Certainly I can." Then get busy and find out how to do it.
- Enthusiasm is the greatest asset in the world. It beats money, power and influence.
- A person that has a good sense of humor has nothing to fear from the world.
- I hear, I forget, I see, I remember, I do, I understand.
- You get treated in life the way you teach people to treat you.
- These are the good old days.
- You are as happy as you make up your mind to be.
- Do people that know you want to be just like you?

- People want to know how much you care before they care how much you know.
- Life: taken by the inch (day), it's a cinch. Taken by the mile (year), it's a trial.
- Being happy is the greatest asset any of us can have.
- I am not getting older. I am chronologically blessed.
- You are my kind of people!
- My good wife, Donna, told a friend when I was out of town that I would visit home next week. I was gone a lot.

STAY POSITIVE!

"A Tribute to my Friend, Jerry Otteson"
by Rev. Dennis Episcopo from Appleton Alliance Church
Delivered at a downtown Appleton Rotary Meeting on Tuesday May 1, 2012.

I'd like to honor a fellow Rotarian today and say thank you to him and also to thank God for him. My friend is Jerry Otteson and I'd like to read some thoughts I've written down on why I appreciate Jerry and want to honor him today.

Dennis Episcopo

I came to Rotary in 1997. Jerry was one of the first Rotarian's I met here. He told me the first time I met him that it was important I meet him because he was Norwegian. I didn't know what that meant at the time, but I do now. In Jerry's world, there are two kinds of people... Norwegians and people who <u>wish</u> they were Norwegians.

Jerry always has an encouraging word for me... always! Most of you have heard his famous stories and jokes... like:

> "I'm not handy around the house - the other day I cut myself on the plunger."
> "You know why Norwegians like lightening? It's because they think they're having their picture taken."

Jerry has taught me a lot about life. Some of his sage mottos will be with me forever... like:

> "Make me feel good and I'll produce."
> "It doesn't matter how smart you are - if nobody likes you."
> "If you're nice to people - you're already a success."

The story I will remember the most, of all the stories Jerry tells, is the one about his dad and the first time he told his dad he was going to be a CUTCO salesman. That seems to have been a very profound and deep moment in Jerry's life. Jerry really loved his dad and respected him. (People look for a dad's blessing)

Jerry went to his dad just after he was accepted by CUTCO and looked for his father's blessing. His dad said,

> "<u>Nobody</u>... <u>nobody</u>... can make a living selling knives... <u>nobody</u>!!"

Jerry said, "I felt like a whipped puppy." I went upstairs and told Bernice (his wife) what my father had said. I told Bernice I was going to quit. She gave me five words that saved my life: <u>"why don't you show him!"</u>

Jerry... you have given myself and lots of other people in this room something that gives life to us every day no matter how mundane our day is. It can be said in five words: <u>"You always make us laugh."</u> Thanks Jerry. We love you. (Let's pray)

Prayer: "Lord, I thank You for Jerry's life and the way You hard-wired him. You've done it! You've made him to be <u>an encourager</u>, someone who <u>not</u> only is positive about <u>his</u> life, but also seeks to be a <u>cheerleader</u> for everyone else's life. May you continue to bless us with Jerry and give him many, many more years as our good friend. We pray in Your Great Name, Amen.